Oxford Primary Illustrated Science Dictionary

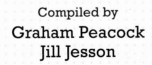

Compiled by
Graham Peacock
Jill Jesson

OXFORD
UNIVERSITY PRESS

OXFORD
UNIVERSITY PRESS

Great Clarendon Street, Oxford, OX2 6DP, United Kingdom

Oxford University Press is a department of the University of Oxford.
It furthers the University's objective of excellence in research,
scholarship, and education by publishing worldwide. Oxford is a
registered trade mark of Oxford University Press in the UK and in
certain other countries

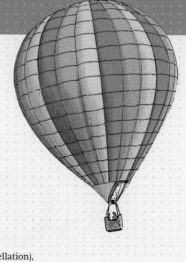

British Library Cataloguing in Publication Data

Data available

ISBN: 978 0 19 277246 6
10 9 8 7 6 5 4 3 2 1

Printed in China

Paper used in the production of this book is a natural,
recyclable product made from wood grown in sustainable forests.
The manufacturing process conforms to the environmental
regulations of the country of origin.

The publishers would like to thank Andrew Delahunty,
lexicographer, for his contribution to this edition.

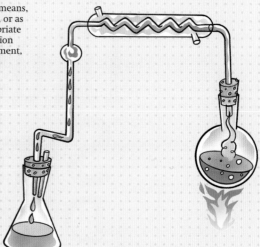

Oxford OWL

For school
Discover eBooks, inspirational
resources, advice and support

For home
Helping your child's learning
with free eBooks, essential
tips and fun activities

www.oxfordowl.co.uk

Oxford Corpus

You can trust this dictionary
to be up to date, relevant
and engaging because
it is powered by the
Oxford Corpus, a unique
living database of children's
and adults' language.

Contents

Introduction

The *Oxford Primary Illustrated Science Dictionary* contains over 1000 words and phrases in alphabetical order with clear definitions and related words which help to build subject vocabulary in young learners.

With words from the curriculum, everyday words from the physical and natural worlds as well as more detailed vocabulary associated with plants, animals, the environment and the human body, this book is designed to be a comprehensive quick reference guide for both the classroom and the home.

catch words

show the first and last word on the page and guide you to the correct place to find the word you need

headword

is in alphabetical order, in blue

related words panel

points you to other words that help to explain this word or build more knowledge in this topic area

derivative

shows you an additional word from the same family as the headword

cross-reference

points you to the main entry which gives you the definition of the word

A B C D E F G H I J K L M N O P Q R S T U V W X Y Z

chart

A chart shows the graphical representation of data. The data may be shown as lines, bars or symbols.

○ **bar chart**

A bar chart shows the data in bars. They may be horizontal or vertical.

○ **line chart**

A line chart shows the data points linked by a line.

○ **pie chart**

A pie chart shows the data in slices.

○ **scattergram chart**

A scattergram shows data from two variables.

line chart

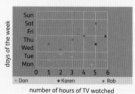

proportion of animals on the farm

pie chart

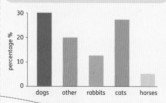

percentage of children in a school who own pets

bar chart

number of hours of TV watched

scattergram chart

chemical

A chemical is a substance from which things are made. Chemicals may be naturally occurring in plants, rocks and animals or made in a laboratory or factory.

• Some foods have **chemicals** added to keep them fresh.

see also carbon, cell, compound, element, hydrogen, oxygen

chemical change *see* change

chemistry

Chemistry is the study of materials and the way they change when they react together.

see also chemical, react

➤ **chemist**

A chemist is a person who studies chemistry.

• **Chemists** can purify a liquid by distilling it.

chicken pox *see* childhood illness

28

4

Where a word has several meanings, different meanings are numbered and often other related words are listed. This is a great way to build and extend vocabulary. Green and yellow panels bring together in one place words that are related to the headword or can be used together with it to talk or write about a topic. Illustrations also help to explain the meaning.

The thematic supplement explores in more detail some of the key scientific terms and concepts in focus areas, including energy, chemicals, the history of life and the solar system.

Word Build panel
shows other words which work together with the headword in the same topic area

pronunciation
shows how to say the word (not how to spell it)

other related words
point you to other words that help to explain this word or build more knowledge in this topic area

alphabet
the alphabet is given on every page with the letter you are in highlighted so you can find your way around the dictionary easily

definition
shows what the word means and if a word has more than one meaning, then each meaning is numbered

illustration
helps to show the meaning of the word

childhood illness

Childhood illnesses are diseases which are most commonly suffered by children. They are less often suffered by adults.

● ● WORD BUILD

➤ **chicken pox**

Chicken pox is a mild but common childhood illness caused by a virus. It rarely needs treatment. The patient is often covered in itchy spots.

see also virus

➤ **measles**

Measles is a common childhood illness caused by a virus. Patients may have a fever and a red rash.

• *People can be immunised against measles.*

see also immunise, virus

➤ **mumps**

Mumps is an infectious disease caused by a virus. Patients may have a swollen face while they are ill.

see also virus

➤ **whooping cough**

Whooping cough is a childhood illness where the patients make long loud coughs.

chimpanzee

A chimpanzee is a primate and a mammal. They are a type of ape closely related to humans.

chitin (*say* **kai**-tin)

Chitin is a tough substance that makes up the external structure of insects. This is called an exoskeleton. Chitin is also found in the exoskeleton of crabs.

see also insect, skeleton, crab

chlorophyll

The green of plant leaves is due to a chemical called chlorophyll. Plants need chlorophyll to photosynthesise.

• *Green leaves contain **chlorophyll**. In the autumn, the leaves of many trees lose their **chlorophyll**.*

see also photosynthesis

chromosome

A chromosome is a strand of material in a plant or animal cell that tells the body how to develop. Chromosomes are made of genes.

nucleus
cell
chromosome
genes

see also cell, gene, nucleus

a
b
c
d
e
f
g
h
i
j
k
l
m
n
o
p
q
r
s
t
u
v
w
x
y
z

Aa

abdomen

The abdomen is the body part that in most animals is between the lungs and the legs. It contains the digestive organs (gut). Indigestion is an abdominal pain.

• *An insect's **abdomen** is at the end of its body.*

abdomen

see also gut, insect, intestine

absorb

To absorb is to soak something up.

• *The kitchen towel **absorbs** liquid, but the table top doesn't.*

➤ absorbent

Absorbent means that a material is able to soak up liquids.

accelerate

To accelerate is to go faster and faster.

• *A rocket **accelerates** away from the launch pad.*

accurate

To be accurate is to be exactly right.

➤ accuracy

The accuracy of something is how correct it is.

acid

An acid is a chemical that has a sour taste. Plaque on teeth produces acid, which attacks tooth enamel.

• *Lemons contain citric **acid**.*

see also alkali, chemical

acid rain

Acid rain is a kind of pollution. It is caused by certain gases which come from the chimneys of factories and power stations, and from the engines of cars and other vehicles.

acids are formed

waste gases

acid falls as rain

see also pollution

adapt

To adapt is to change. Groups of plants or animals adapt over time to suit their surroundings.

• *An anteater's long nose and sticky tongue are **adapted** for poking into anthills and licking up ants.*

see also environment

➤ adaptation

Adaptation is how a group of animals or plants change to suit their environment.

addict

An addict is someone who has a habit they can't give up.

DON'T MESS WITH DRUGS

YOU MAY BECOME ADDICTED!

KICK YOUR ADDICTION!

ALCOHOLICS ARE ADDICTED TO DRINK!

see also alcohol, caffeine, heroin, nicotine

➤ addiction

An addiction is a habit which is very hard to give up.

adult

The adult is the mature form of a plant or animal.

aerobic

Aerobic exercise makes you breathe deeply. It means there is a good supply of oxygen to the muscles.

see also exercise, muscle, oxygen

aerobic exercise see exercise

a
b
c
d
e
f
g
h
i
j
k
l
m
n
o
p
q
r
s
t
u
v
w
x
y
z

aerodynamic

When an object is aerodynamic it slips through the air easily.

• *Wind tunnels are used to test the air resistance of vehicles to see whether they are **aerodynamic**.*

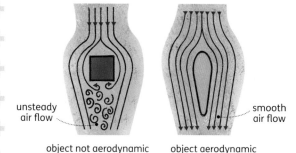

unsteady air flow   smooth air flow

object not aerodynamic   object aerodynamic

see also air resistance

AIDS

AIDS stands for Acquired Immune Deficiency Syndrome. It is caused by a virus called HIV. HIV weakens the body and this lets in many other infections. It is a disease that can be caught during sexual intercourse.

• ***AIDS** can affect men and women of any age or nationality.*

see also disease, germ, sexual intercourse, virus, infect

air

Air is the gas that we breathe. Air is a mixture of different gases, mostly nitrogen and oxygen. Other gases in air include argon and carbon dioxide.

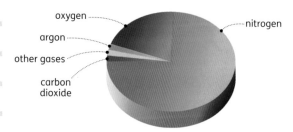

oxygen

argon

other gases

carbon dioxide

nitrogen

see also atmosphere, carbon dioxide, nitrogen, oxygen, gas

air resistance *see* resistance

alcohol

Alcohol is a liquid that is part of many drinks. The alcohol in beer and wine can make people drunk. It is illegal to sell alcohol to people under 18 years old.

see also ferment

algae *(say* al-gee)

Algae are simple green plants that do not have roots. Some kinds form the green slime on paths and in ponds.

• *Seaweeds are **algae** that live in the sea.*

see also plant, root

alien

❶ An alien plant or animal is one which is living out of its usual habitat.

• *The giraffe is an **alien** in a polar environment.*

OPPOSITE The opposite of alien is indigenous.

NORTH POLE

see also habitat, indigenous

❷ Living things that are thought to come from another planet are aliens.

alimentary canal

The long tube from mouth to anus is called the alimentary canal.

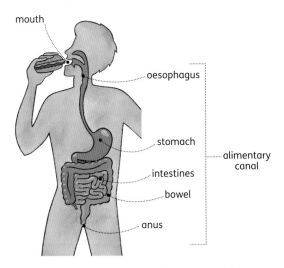

mouth
oesophagus
stomach
alimentary canal
intestines
bowel
anus

see also anus, bowel, gut, intestine, mouth, oesophagus, stomach

alive

Living things are alive. They can grow, breathe, reproduce, move, feed and excrete waste material.

OPPOSITE The opposite of alive is dead.

reproducing

moving

feeding

excreting

see also excrete, life, reproduction

alkali

An alkali is the chemical opposite of an acid. Strong alkalis like bleach are dangerous.

see also acid, chemical

allergy

An allergy occurs when the body reacts badly to a substance. Allergies often produce a skin rash or cause sneezing.

• *Hay fever is caused by an* **allergy** *to pollen.*

see also pollen

alloy

A mixture of two metals is called an alloy.

• *Trumpets are made of brass, an* **alloy** *of copper and zinc.*

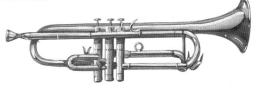

see also metal

aluminium

Aluminium is a lightweight, silvery, non-magnetic metal that is used to make many things.

• *Aeroplanes are made from* **aluminium** *because it is light and strong.*

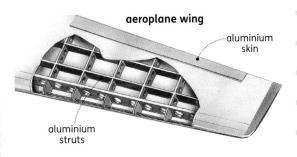

aeroplane wing

aluminium skin

aluminium struts

see also metal

ammonite

An ammonite was a type of animal which is now extinct. It lived in the sea at the time of the dinosaurs.

• **Ammonites** *are found as fossils in rocks.*

see also dinosaur, extinct, fossil,

amount

An amount is a quantity of something.

• *The* **amount** *of yeast needed to make bread is found in a bread recipe.*

amp (*also* Amp)

The unit for measuring the flow of electric current is an amp. It is short for ampere.

• *Plugs for heaters are fitted with 13-***Amp** *fuses while lights have 3-***Amp** *fuses.*

amphibian

An amphibian lays its eggs in water and the young at first breathe through gills. Later they develop lungs and live on land and in water. Frogs, newts and toads are all amphibians.

• **Amphibians** *begin life as tadpoles.*

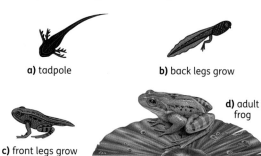

a) tadpole   **b)** back legs grow

c) front legs grow   **d)** adult frog

see also air, breathe, egg, gill, metamorphosis, frog

amplify

When you amplify a sound it is made louder.

• *When the guitarist turns up the volume, the sound is* **amplified.**

see also sound

anaesthetic

An anaesthetic is a chemical that stops humans or animals feeling pain.

• *Vets and doctors use* **anaesthetics** *on their patients.*

see also chemical

analyse

To analyse is to look at all parts of something in detail in order to understand it.

• *Scientists* **analyse** *all parts of their tests and experiments to see what has been learned.*

see also scientist, fair test, experiment

ancestor

An ancestor is the form of a plant or animal which lived in the past and from which it is descended.

animal

An animal is a living thing which has senses. Animals can move some part of themselves. Unlike plants they cannot make their own food and have to eat plants or other animals.

• *An **animal** eats, breathes, reproduces itself, moves, is sensitive to its environment and eventually dies.*

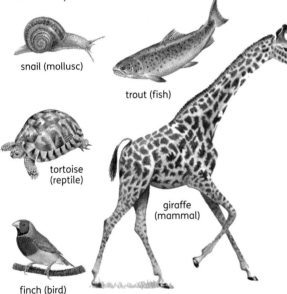

snail (mollusc)

trout (fish)

tortoise (reptile)

giraffe (mammal)

finch (bird)

see *also* life processes, plant, senses

annual

❶ An annual is a type of plant which lives, flowers, makes seed and dies in one year.

• *Cress is an **annual** plant which is often eaten.*

see *also* plant, seed

❷ Annual events happen every year, such as an annual migration.

anther

The anther is the pollen-producing male part of a plant. Anthers grow on the end of long thin stalks called filaments. An anther and a filament taken together are called a stamen.

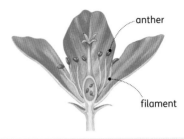

anther

filament

see *also* flower, male, pollen, stamen

antibiotic

An antibiotic is a medicine that kills bacteria. Antibiotics cannot kill viruses so are not useful for treating colds.

see *also* bacterium, cold, virus

antiseptic

An antiseptic is a substance that kills germs in cuts and wounds. If you do not kill germs they can cause cuts to go septic.

• ***Antiseptics** come as liquids, creams and sprays.*

see *also* germ, septic

anus

The anus is the hole at the end of the alimentary canal through which waste food is pushed out.

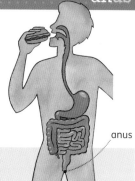

anus

see also **alimentary canal**

ape

Apes are related to humans. Types of ape are gorillas, chimps and orangutans.

appendix

The appendix is a small part of the intestine which in some animals helps to digest tough vegetation.

arachnid

An arachnid is an invertebrate that has eight legs. Spiders and scorpions are arachnids.

• *All* **arachnids** *are arthropods.*

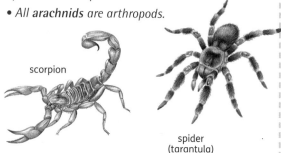

scorpion

spider
(tarantula)

see also **arthropod, invertebrate, insect, spider**

argument

An argument is an exchange of ideas.

artery

An artery is a blood vessel that carries blood away from the heart. Most arteries contain blood that is rich in oxygen.

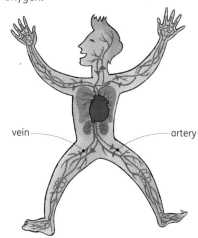

vein

artery

see also **capillary, heart, vein**

arthropod

An arthropod is an animal that has jointed legs and a hard outer skeleton instead of bones. Insects, spiders, crustaceans and woodlice are all arthropods.

• *Arthropods do not have bony skeletons.*

garden spider
(arachnid)

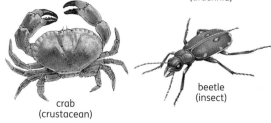

crab
(crustacean)

beetle
(insect)

see also **arachnid, crustacean, insect, crab, myriapod**

asexual reproduction
see **reproduction**

asteroid
An asteroid is a rocky or metal object that orbits the Sun. The biggest of them is about the size of Britain. Most are tiny. Most asteroids are found in the asteroid belt between Mars and Jupiter.

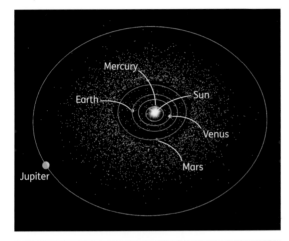

see also **metal, orbit, rock, Sun**

asthma
Asthma is a condition where the airways in the lungs close up, making it difficult to breathe. Some people's asthma gets worse when they breathe in cigarette smoke. Medicines to help asthma are usually breathed in through a device called an inhaler.

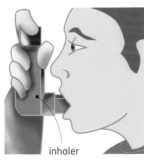

inhaler

see also **lung**

astronaut
An astronaut is a person who travels into space.

astronomy
The study of the stars and planets is called astronomy.

see also **planet, star, universe, galaxy**

➤ **astronomer**
An astronomer is someone who studies stars and planets.

atmosphere
The atmosphere is the air that surrounds planet Earth.

• *The **atmosphere** has several layers.*

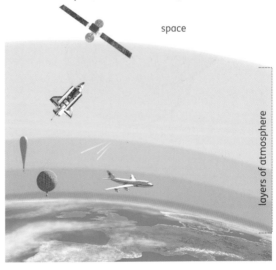

space

layers of atmosphere

see also **air, Earth, planet**

A
B
C
D
E
F
G
H
I
J
K
L
M
N
O
P
Q
R
S
T
U
V
W
X
Y
Z

atom

An atom is the smallest particle of an element. Each atom has a nucleus in the middle, and one or more electrons going round it.

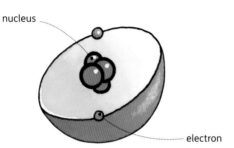

nucleus

electron

see also electron, element, nucleus, particle

attract

To attract is to bring something closer.

• *A magnet **attracts** magnetic materials.*

see also magnet, pole

axis (*plural* axes)

The axis of the Earth is an imaginary line through the Earth from the north pole to the south pole. The Earth rotates around its axis.

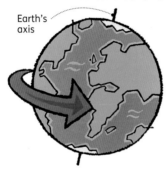

Earth's axis

see also Earth, season

Bb

bacterium (*plural* bacteria)

A bacterium is a tiny living thing. Some cause illness such as diarrhoea and earache. Others are used to help make compost, cheese and yoghurt.

• ***Bacteria** can infect many parts of the body.*

see also antibiotic, germ, infection, infect

balance

When two forces are equal they balance each other. The weight of a floating object is balanced by upthrust from the water.

• *This seesaw isn't **balanced** because one person is heavier than the other.*

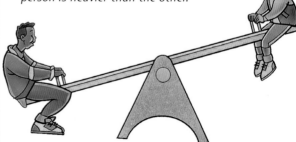

see also centre of gravity, float, pivot, force

bar chart see chart

bar graph see graph

bark

Bark is the outer
covering of a tree.
The bark prevents
disease from entering
the wood of the tree.

bark

see also tree, disease

bar magnet see magnet

barometer

Barometers are devices that show air pressure.
High pressure usually means fine weather.
Low pressure gives windy wet weather.

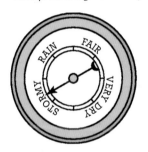

RAIN FAIR VERY DRY STORMY

see also pressure

bat

A bat is a flying mammal. Its wings are thin skin
stretched between its fingers and its leg.

• Small **bats** eat insects. Larger **bats** eat fruit.
Vampire **bats** drink blood.

battery

A battery is a group of cells. Batteries contain
chemicals that produce electricity in a circuit

• There are many different types of **battery**.

see also cell, chemical, circuit, current,
electricity, volt

beak

The hard mouthparts of birds and some reptiles
is called a beak. Beaks are made of a material
called chitin.

• Birds have different types of **beak**, depending on
what they eat.

curlew

pelican

finch

flamingo

eagle

see also bird, reptile

bee

A bee is a flying insect known for its role in
pollination. Bees make honey to feed to their larvae.
It is stored in a wax honeycomb. Bees can sting.

• There are many types of **bee**. Most live in
colonies. Some are solitary.

a b c d e f g h i j k l m n o p q r s t u v w x y z

A B C D E F G H I J K L M N O P Q R S T U V W X Y Z

beetle

A beetle is an insect with hard wing cases covering its back.

• *The ladybird, the dung* **beetle** *and the rhinoceros* **beetle** *are just three of the 300,000 different types of* **beetle** *in the world.*

diving beetle

ground beetle

tiger beetle

see also insect

berry

A fleshy fruit with a seed in it is a berry. Berries are often edible so animals help to disperse the seeds when eating them.

• *Cherries and blackcurrants are* **berries.**

see also seed dispersal

bicarbonate of soda

Bicarbonate of soda is a chemical that fizzes when mixed with water. It is used in self-raising flour to produce light cakes.

see also chemical, irreversible change

biennial

❶ A plant which germinates one year and flowers the next is said to be biennial.

foxgloves

see also germinate, plant, seed

❷ Something which happens every two years is biennial.

Big Bang

The universe started with a huge explosion. Scientists call it the Big Bang.

• *Everything that makes up the planets and stars was created soon after the* **Big Bang.**

see also planet, star, universe

binocular

Animals with binocular vision, such as people and owls, have two eyes looking forward.

• *Animals with* **binocular** *vision can judge distances accurately.*

see also animal, eye

biodegradable

Materials that break down and decay are biodegradable. Leaves and branches are biodegradable. Most plastic is not biodegradable but some is specially made to break down eventually.

see also **decay**

biodiversity

Biodiversity refers to the variety of plants and animals in the world or in a habitat.

• *Plants and animals need an environment which has a rich **biodiversity** so that they do not become dependent on a single species which may become diseased or die out.*

see also **habitat, indigenous, plant, animal**

➤ **biodiverse**

We use the term biodiverse to describe a habitat or environment which has a wide range of plants and animals.

biology

Biology is the study of plants, animals and other living things.

see also **botany, life processes, zoology, plant, animal**

biped

An animal that walks on two legs is a biped. This is known as being bipedal.

• *Humans are the only mammals which move as **bipeds** all the time.*

see also **animal, bird**

a
b
c
d
e
f
g
h
i
j
k
l
m
n
o
p
q
r
s
t
u
v
w
x
y
z

bird

A bird is a two-legged animal covered with feathers. All birds have wings but not all can fly. Ostriches and penguins, for example, cannot fly.

• *All birds lay eggs, and many birds build nests.*

blue tit

weaver bird and nest

thrush

tern

emperor penguin

swan

gull

goose

duck

see also egg, feather

black hole

Black holes are the remains of giant stars that have collapsed. Anything that comes close to a black hole is attracted in and is never seen again.

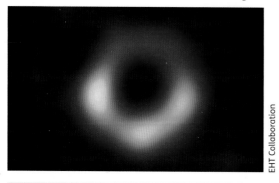

EHT Collaboration

see also mass, star

bladder

The bladder is an organ in the abdomen. Urine is stored there.

• *Urine travels to the bladder from the kidneys.*

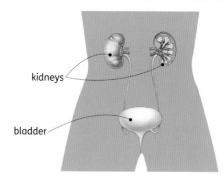

kidneys

bladder

see also abdomen, organ, urine

blood

Blood is the red liquid that is pumped around our body by the heart. It carries oxygen, food and water to all the parts of our body.

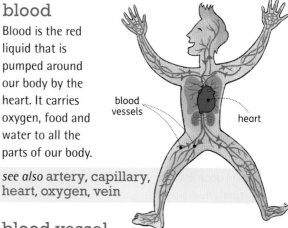

blood vessels

heart

see also artery, capillary, heart, oxygen, vein

blood vessel

A blood vessel is a tube through which blood flows round the body. Blood vessels are part of the circulatory system.

see also circulatory system, heart, artery, vein

body

All living things have a body. All life processes happen inside the body. Bodies are made from plant or animal cells.

see also cell, living, life processes

boil

When a liquid is heated to a particular temperature it will boil and evaporate. At boiling point, bubbles of vapour are released. Water boils at 100°C.

• *When a liquid **boils**, bubbles are formed in all parts of the liquid.*

see also gas, liquid, vapour, evaporate

boiling point

Boiling point is the temperature at which a liquid evaporates and becomes a gas. The boiling point for water is 100°C.

bone

Bone is a hard and stiff material. It is made mainly from the chemical calcium phosphate.

• *In the middle of some **bones** there is soft material called **bone** marrow.*

●●● WORD BUILD

➤ femur

The femur is the bone in your thigh.

➤ fibula

The bone below the knee of a human is the fibula. It is the outer and smaller bone in the lower hind leg of a four-legged animal.

➤ humerus

The bone connecting your elbow and your shoulder is called the humerus.

➤ radius

The radius is the bone in your arm on the same side as your thumb.

➤ ribs

The ribs are part of the skeleton of all vertebrates. They are bones which protect the organs. They are attached to the spine.

see also vertebrate　　》

➤ skull

The skull is the name for the bones of the head. This includes the jaw.

➤ tibia

The large inner bone in the shin of a mammal is its tibia.

➤ ulna

The ulna is the bone in your arm on the opposite side to your thumb.

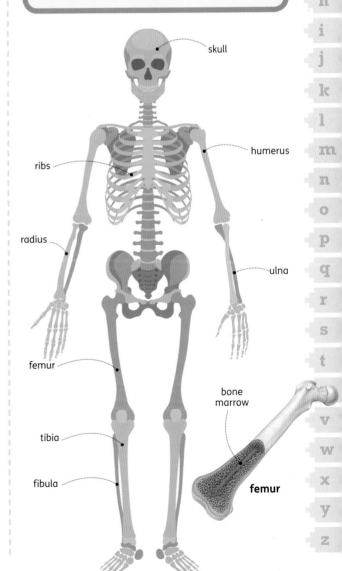

a b c d e f g h i j k l m n o p q r s t u v w x y z

A B C D E F G H I J K L M N O P Q R S T U V W X Y Z

botany

Botany is the study of plants.

flower
petal
stem
leaf
bud
root

see also biology, plant

bowel

Bowel is a name for the lower part of the intestines.

• The faeces pass through the **bowel**.

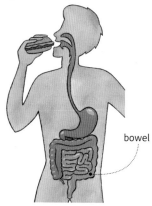

bowel

see also alimentary canal, intestine

brain

The brain is a mass of nerve tissue. It is the organ we use to think.

• Different parts of the **brain** do different jobs.

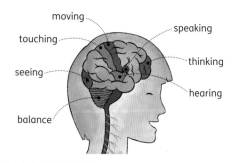

moving
speaking
touching
thinking
seeing
hearing
balance

see also nerve, organ, tissue

brake

A brake is something which applies friction to a moving object

• Bikes have **brakes** to slow them down.

see also friction

breathe

Animals breathe by taking in air. They use oxygen from the air to help them get energy from food. Animals get rid of another gas, carbon dioxide, as they breathe out.

• Blowing out a candle involves **breathing** out.

see also carbon dioxide, oxygen, respiration

breed

When living things breed, they produce young.

parents

breeding

young

see also reproduction

brick

Brick is a manufactured building material made from baked clay.

• *When clay is heated to a high temperature to make **bricks**, an irreversible change makes it hard.*

see also clay, change

brightness

Brightness refers to the amount of power in a light. Brightness is measured in lumens.

brittle

Materials that are brittle do not bend easily. They snap or break into pieces.

• *Pottery is strong, but **brittle**.*

see also glass

bud

The bud is the part of the plant which contains new leaves or flowers.

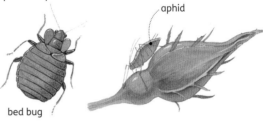

bud

see also leaf, flower

bug

A bug is an insect with sucking mouthparts.

• *The bed **bug** sucks blood and the aphid sucks plant sap.*

aphid

bed bug

see also insect

bulb

❶ A bulb is a short underground stem surrounded by thick, swollen leaves that stores food for the plant.

• *Onion plants have **bulbs**. The onion leaves are folded inside the swollen **bulb**.*

leaves

see also plant

❷ An electric bulb is device which produces light when electricity passes through it.

a
b
f
g
h
i
j
k
l
m
n
o
p
q
r
s
t
u
v
w
x
y
z

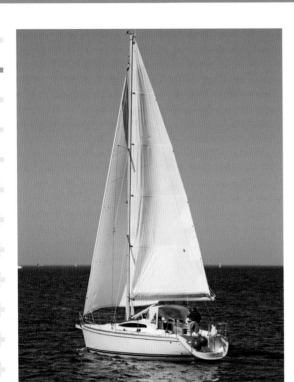

buoyancy

Buoyancy refers to the upward force acting on a solid which is in a liquid. The upthrust balances the weight of the object.

• *Boats float because of the **buoyancy** from the water.*

see also upthrust, liquid, displace

burn

To burn is to be on fire. When a chemical burns it produces a flame. The burning chemical combines with oxygen from the air.

• *The wax is **burning** and combining with oxygen to produce carbon dioxide.*

see also carbon dioxide, chemical, oxygen, air

button magnet *see* magnet

buzzer

A buzzer is a device which makes a buzzing sound when it is part of a circuit.

see also circuit

Cc

cactus (*plural* cacti)

A cactus is a spiky plant that lives in very dry areas.

• *Cacti have thick stems to store water. Many have spikes instead of leaves.*

caffeine

Caffeine is a drug found in coffee, some soft drinks, and tea.

• *Caffeine in coffee and tea might stop you sleeping well at night.*

see also drug

calcium

Calcium is one of the chemicals that form our bones and teeth.

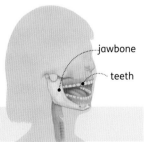

see also bone, tooth, chemical

calibrate

To calibrate is to mark an instrument with a standard scale of measurements.

• *Rulers are **calibrated** on a standard scale so that all measurements with them will be comparable.*

➤ calibration

A calibration is a scale marked on a measuring device such as a jug or ruler.

calorie

The calorie is the unit that measures the amount of energy in food. A 10-year-old boy needs about 2,400 calories of food energy each day.

• *Eating more **calories** than you use can make you overweight.*

see also energy, kilojoule

calyx

The calyx is the green outer covering of a flower bud.

• *The **calyx** is made up of sepals.*

sepals

see also flower, sepal

camera

A camera is a device for taking photographs, films or television pictures. Digital cameras record pictures using computer chips.

• *Cameras can be used for portraits, for medicine, for spying and to make films.*

see also lens, light

camouflage

Camouflage colouring on an animal helps it to blend into its background so it is hard to see. An animal that matches its background is camouflaged.

• *These insects are **camouflaged** in leaves and twigs.*

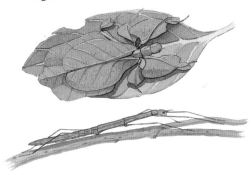

cancer

Cancer is an illness caused when cells in the body begin to grow in an unusual way.

• ***Cancers** can be treated with medicines and radiation.*

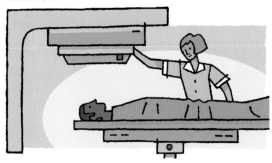

see also **cell, radiation, reproduction**

canine *see* **tooth**

cannabis

Cannabis is a plant. It contains drugs. It is also called grass, hash, dagga or dope.

• ***Cannabis** contains drugs that affect the brain.*

see also **drug, addict**

capillary

A capillary is a small blood vessel. There are huge numbers of capillaries in our bodies. They are very thin and tiny amounts of blood flow through them.

• ***Capillaries** in the lungs collect oxygen from the air and take it back to the heart.*

see also **artery, blood, vein**

carbohydrate

The carbohydrate food group is one of the main food groups. Carbohydrates give us energy.

• ***Carbohydrates** come from sugars, starches and fibre and are found in fruits, grains, vegetables and milk products.*

pasta

sugar

wheaty pops

cereal

maize

bread

potato

see also **energy**

carbon

Carbon is an element. Our bodies are partly made up from carbon.

• *Diamonds, soot, coal, and the graphite in pencil leads are all forms of **carbon**.*

see also **chemical, coal, diamond, element, graphite**

carbon cycle

All living things contain carbon. When they die, the carbon is recycled to make new living things. Fossil fuels come from the remains of dead plants and animals. When burned, the carbon in coal or oil is returned to the atmosphere. This is called the carbon cycle.

see also carbon, fossil fuel, coal, dead, oil

carbon dioxide

Carbon dioxide is a gas. It is a compound made from carbon and oxygen. It is the gas that humans and animals breathe out.

• *Carbon dioxide can be used to put out fires.*

see also breathe, compound, oxygen

carnivore

A carnivore is an animal that eats other animals.

• *Tigers, vultures and spiders are all carnivores.*

see also food chain

cast

We can make a cast of a foot or paw print by pressing it into something soft and filling the impression with wet plaster. When the plaster sets a cast is formed.

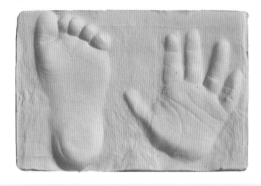

see also fossil, solution

caterpillar

A caterpillar is the larva of a butterfly or a moth. The caterpillar hatches from a tiny egg. When it has grown big enough, it becomes a chrysalis (pupa).

• *Caterpillars of the peacock butterfly eat nettle leaves.*

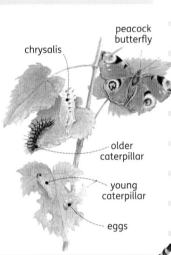

chrysalis

peacock butterfly

older caterpillar

young caterpillar

eggs

see also chrysalis, insect, larva, life cycle, metamorphosis, pupa

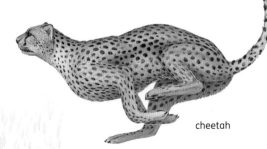

cheetah

cause

To cause something means to make it happen.

• *Heating bread **causes** it to become dry and may even **cause** it to become toast.*

celestial

Celestial means to do with the sky or space, or relating to astronomy.

see also astronomy

➤ celestial body

A celestial body is any naturally occurring object in space, which is seen from the Earth.

• *Stars, planets and asteroids are **celestial** bodies.*

cell

❶ The smallest part of a living thing is a cell. All living things are made up of cells. Most cells have a nucleus and a cell wall. Each organ in the body is made from a different type of cell.

• *Plant **cells** have a tough **cell** wall, animal **cells** do not.*

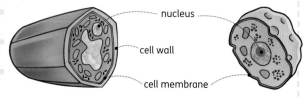

plant cell **animal cell**

nucleus

cell wall

cell membrane

see also muscle, nucleus, skin, body

❷ An electric cell is a device that produces electrical current by a chemical reaction. Several cells make up a battery.

• *Electric **cells** have different shapes for different uses.*

see also battery

Celsius

Temperature is measured in degrees Celsius (°C).

• *The freezing point of water is 0°C and its boiling point is 100°C.*

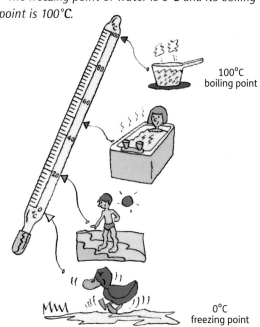

100°C
boiling point

0°C
freezing point

see also boil, freeze, thermometer

centre of gravity

The centre of gravity of an object is the point around which it balances.

• *Objects with a low **centre of gravity** are very stable. Objects with a high **centre of gravity** fall over easily.*

high centre
of gravity

low centre
of gravity

see also balance, gravity

ceramic

A ceramic material is made of hardened clay.

• *China cups and flower pots are types of ceramic.*

see also clay

cereal

A cereal is a type of grass plant whose seeds give us food. Plants such as oats, wheat, rice, maize and barley are cereals.

• *Cereals are all types of grass.*

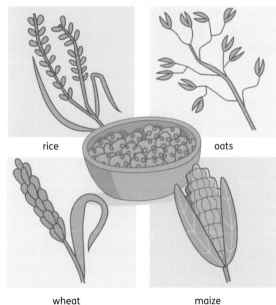

rice

oats

wheat

maize

see also grass

chalk

Chalk is a white rock made from the remains of tiny sea creatures. Chalk was laid down millions of years ago, at the time of the dinosaurs.

• *In some places chalk forms tall cliffs.*

see also dinosaur, rock

change

❶ If something changes it does not stay the same.

• *Some leaves change colour in autumn.*

❷ A change is when something does not stay the same.

• *A change of diet may help someone lose weight.*

> ### ⚙ reversible change
>
> An action which can be undone is reversible. A reversible change is a change that does not alter the chemical make-up of a substance. For example, the melting of ice is a reversible change as the water can be refrozen.
>
> ### ⚙ irreversible change
>
> An action which cannot be undone is irreversible. When substances are combined to make a new material and the original substances cannot be brought back, this is an irreversible change. Burning and rotting produce irreversible changes.

change of state

A change of state occurs when a solid changes into a liquid, or a liquid becomes a gas, or a gas becomes a liquid, or a liquid becomes a solid.

• *There is a change of state when water changes into ice or water vapour.*

see also water, ice, vapour, freeze, melt, evaporate, condense

characteristic

A characteristic of something is what helps to identify it.

charcoal

Charcoal is the remains of partly burnt wood. To make charcoal, wood is heated in a container that has very little air in it.

• *Charcoal leaves a black mark on paper. Artists sometimes use it for drawing.*

see also air, burn, wood

a
b
c
d
e
f
g
h
i
j
k
l
m
n
o
p
q
r
s
t
u
v
w
x
y
z

chart

A chart shows the graphical representation of data. The data may be shown as lines, bars or symbols.

○ bar chart

A bar chart shows the data in bars. They may be horizontal or vertical.

○ line chart

A line chart shows the data points linked by a line.

○ pie chart

A pie chart shows the data in slices.

○ scattergram chart

A scattergram shows data from two variables.

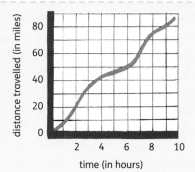

line chart

proportion of animals on the farm

pie chart

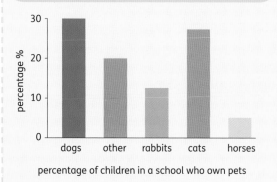

percentage of children in a school who own pets

bar chart

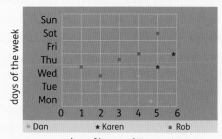

number of hours of TV watched

scattergram chart

chemical

A chemical is a substance from which things are made. Chemicals may be naturally occurring in plants, rocks and animals or made in a laboratory or factory.

• *Some foods have **chemicals** added to keep them fresh.*

see also chemical, cell, compound, element, hydrogen, oxygen

chemical change *see* change

chemistry

Chemistry is the study of materials and the way they change when they react together.

see also chemical, react

➤ **chemist**

A chemist is a person who studies chemistry.

• ***Chemists** can purify a liquid by distilling it.*

chicken pox *see* childhood illness

childhood illness

Childhood illnesses are diseases which are most commonly suffered by children. They are less often suffered by adults.

WORD BUILD

➤ **chicken pox**

Chicken pox is a mild but common childhood illness caused by a virus. It rarely needs treatment. The patient is often covered in itchy spots.

see also virus

➤ **measles**

Measles is a common childhood illness caused by a virus. Patients may have a fever and a red rash.

• *People can be immunised against* **measles**.

see also immunise, virus

➤ **mumps**

Mumps is an infectious disease caused by a virus. Patients may have a swollen face while they are ill.

see also virus

➤ **whooping cough**

Whooping cough is a childhood illness where the patients make long loud coughs.

chimpanzee

A chimpanzee is a primate and a mammal. They are a type of ape closely related to humans.

chitin (*say* kai-tin)

Chitin is a tough substance that makes up the external structure of insects. This is called an exoskeleton. Chitin is also found in the exoskeleton of crabs.

see also insect, skeleton, crab

chlorophyll

The green of plant leaves is due to a chemical called chlorophyll. Plants need chlorophyll to photosynthesise.

• *Green leaves contain* **chlorophyll**. *In the autumn, the leaves of many trees lose their* **chlorophyll**.

see also photosynthesis

chromosome

A chromosome is a strand of material in a plant or animal cell that tells the body how to develop. Chromosomes are made of genes.

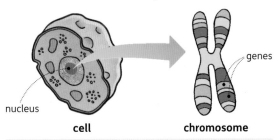

nucleus

genes

cell   **chromosome**

see also cell, gene, nucleus

chrysalis

Chrysalis is another word for pupa.

• *The chrysalis is the resting stage as a caterpillar changes into an adult form of the insect which may be a moth, a fly or a butterfly.*

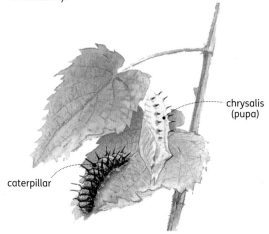

chrysalis (pupa)

caterpillar

see *also* caterpillar, larva, life cycle, metamorphosis

cigarette

A cigarette is a tube of paper filled with tobacco. Many smokers are addicted to the nicotine in tobacco.

see *also* addict, nicotine

circuit

A circuit is a complete path that an electric current can flow around. It must include a source of electricity, such as a battery or cell. Electricity flows from the battery or cell, through wires and devices before returning to the battery or cell.

• *When a circuit is complete electricity can flow. When a circuit is not complete the bulb is not lit.*

see *also* battery, cell, electricity

○ parallel circuit

In a parallel circuit, electricity can take more than one path round a circuit.

see *also* electricity, series circuit

○ series circuit (*also* simple circuit)

An electrical circuit that has only one path through it is called a series circuit or a simple circuit.

see *also* circuit, parallel circuit

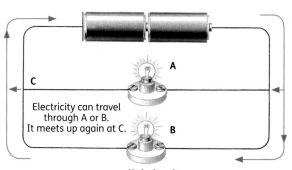

C

A

B

Electricity can travel through A or B. It meets up again at C.

parallel circuit

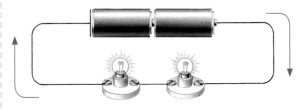

series circuit

circulatory system

The circulatory system is a network of blood vessels and a heart which keep blood that has oxygen in it circulating round (continuously going around) the body.

see *also* blood vessel, artery, vein, heart, oxygen

classification

Classification is the process of sorting things into groups which have something in common.

see also classify

➤ classification keys

Diagrams which help sort items into different groups are called classification keys.

➤ classify

To classify is to sort things into groups.

- *All living things can be classified into groups.*
- *Animals with bones are classified as vertebrates.*
- *Animals with six legs are classified as insects.*
- *Plants with seeds on cones are classified as conifers.*

see also conifer, insect, vertebrate

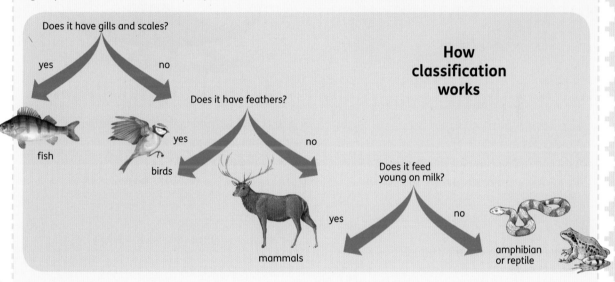

How classification works

Does it have gills and scales?

yes → fish

no → Does it have feathers?

yes → birds

no → Does it feed young on milk?

yes → mammals

no → amphibian or reptile

clay *see* rock

climate

The climate of a place is the most usual weather it has over many years.

- *This desert has a hot, dry climate, but occasionally it has rainy weather.*

see also weather

cloud

A cloud is made up of billions of tiny water drops. These drops fall as rain when they get heavy enough.

- *Dark storm clouds bring rain.*

see also condense

a b c d e f g h i j k l m n o p q r s t u v w x y z

31

A B C D E F G H I J K L M N O P Q R S T U V W X Y Z

coal

Coal is a shiny black rock made from the remains of trees that lived millions of years ago.

• *Coal began to form in swampy forests about 300 million years ago.*

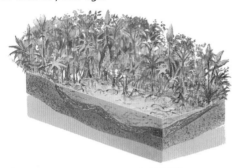

see also carbon, mineral, rock

cocoon

A cocoon is a type of chrysalis or pupa. Cocoons are made from threads that are spun by the caterpillar.

• *Silk comes from the cocoons of silk moth caterpillars. Each has many metres of thread which is used to make silk clothes.*

see also chrysalis, pupa

cold

❶ Cold is the absence of heat.

see also heat

❷ A person with a cold has a runny nose and feels unwell. Colds are caused by a virus.

see also virus, common cold

cold-blooded

Cold-blooded animals cannot keep their bodies warm without heat from the Sun or from their surroundings.

• *Reptiles and fish are cold-blooded.*

sailfish

chameleon

collect

To collect something is to take something to add to a group of objects.

➤ collection

A collection is a group of objects.

colony

A colony is a group of similar animals living together

• *Ants and penguins live in colonies.*

see also bee

colour

White light is composed of more than one colour. It is made of all the colours of the rainbow.

• *A prism can split white light into a spectrum of* **colours**.

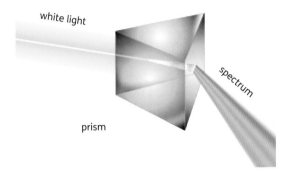

white light

spectrum

prism

see also light, prism, rainbow, spectrum

comet

A comet is a ball of ice orbiting the Sun. From Earth, comets look like bright stars. We can only see the tails on very bright comets.

• *Bright* **comets** *can be seen from the Earth about every ten years.*

see also orbit, Sun

common cold

The common cold is an illness caused by a virus. Patients may have a runny nose, cough, sneeze and have a raised temperature. Colds are spread by droplets of infection from one person to another. To get better, people need to rest, keep warm, and drink plenty of water.

see also virus, infect

communicate

To communicate is to share or exchange information, news and ideas.

• *We can* **communicate** *through activities such as dance, art and sign language.*

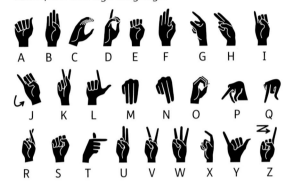

A B C D E F G H I

J K L M N O P Q

R S T U V W X Y Z

➤ communication

Communication is the way living things pass information to each other.

compare

We compare ideas, items and events by looking for similarities and differences.

➤ comparative

If things can be compared they are said to be comparative.

see also chart, graph

compass

A compass needle always points north. The needle is a magnet. It is attracted by the magnetic poles of the Earth.

see also magnetic pole, magnetism

complex

Something which has many different but connected parts is complex.

• *Living organisms are* **complex.** *Ideas can be* **complex** *as well.*

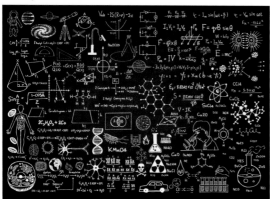

see also experiment, evidence

component

A component is a part of a machine.

compost

Compost is a mixture in which you grow plants. Compost can be made using soil, peat or coconut fibre. Compost can also be made by rotting down garden clippings, and manure from animals.

• *The weed can go on the* **compost** *heap as it will rot. The plastic will not make* **compost.**

see also decay, rot

compound

A combination of two elements is called a compound. Water is a compound made from oxygen and hydrogen. Carbon dioxide is a compound of carbon and oxygen.

• *This drawing shows the way that water is a* **compound** *of hydrogen and oxygen atoms.*

water

hydrogen atoms

oxygen atom

see also atom, carbon, hydrogen, oxygen, element

compress

To compress something is to press or squeeze it by a force so that it takes up less space.

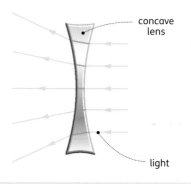

concave

Concave means curved inwards, like the inside of a ball or circle. Mirrors or lenses that dip inwards are called concave.

OPPOSITE The opposite of concave is convex.

concave lens

light

see also convex, lens, mirror, reflect

concentrate

To concentrate a liquid is to make it stronger. A concentrated solution is one where there is a lot of solid dissolved in it.

OPPOSITE The opposite of concentrate is dilute.

see also dilute, solution

➤ concentration

❶ Concentration in a liquid refers to how much solid is dissolved in it.

concentrated juice   dilute juice

❷ Concentration is also thinking hard about something.

conclusion

After an experiment, you should look at your evidence to see what you have found. This is your conclusion.

see also experiment, evidence

concrete

Concrete is a manufactured material made from sand, lime and water.

• *Concrete is a strong material for building bridges and houses.*

see also manufactured, strength

condense

Water vapour will condense on a cold surface, so that it changes from a gas to a liquid.

see also gas, liquid, state of matter

➤ condensation

Condensation happens when water vapour cools and changes state from a gas to a liquid.

• *Running a bath causes **condensation** on the mirror.*

conduct

❶ Materials that conduct electricity allow it to pass through them.

• *All metals **conduct** electricity. Carbon and silicon **conduct** too, but not as well as metals.*

see also electricity

❷ Materials that conduct heat allow heat to pass through them.

• *A metal spoon **conducts** heat.*

see also heat

➤ conductivity

❶ Electrical conductivity occurs in materials which allow an electrical current to pass through them. Wire and plug pins do this.

❷ Thermal conductivity occurs in materials which allow heat to pass through them. Metal radiators are hot to touch.

➤ conductor

❶ Materials that let electricity pass through easily are good conductors of electricity.

❷ Materials that let heat pass through easily are good conductors of heat.

• *All metals are good **conductors** of heat. Wood and plastic are poor **conductors**.*

❸ Materials that let sound pass through easily are good conductors of sound.

a b c d e f g h i j k l m n o p q r s t u v w x y z

A B C D E F G H I J K L M N O P Q R S T U V W X Y Z

conifer

A conifer is a plant that carries its seeds on cones. Most conifers are evergreen.

• *The Scots pine is a **conifer** tree.*

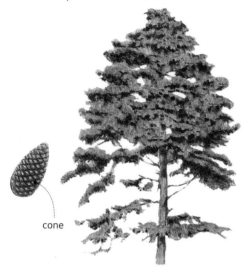

cone

see also deciduous, evergreen, seed

conservation

Trying to stop animals and plants from dying out is known as conservation.

• *All these animals will die out without **conservation**.*

mountain gorilla

panda

tiger

see also extinct, life processes

➤ conservationist

Conservationists are people who try to stop living things becoming extinct.

constellation

A constellation is a pattern of stars in the sky.

• *Stars in a **constellation** may appear to be close but may be many light years apart.*

see also star, light year

constipation

If people have a problem in passing faeces they have constipation.

• *A diet of high-fibre foods like these should help avoid **constipation**.*

see also faeces, fibre

consumer

A consumer is an animal which eats other animals or plants.

• Foxes are **consumers** of mice and blackberries.

see also **producer**

contract

To contract is to become smaller.

• Metals like mercury **contract** when they get cooler.

OPPOSITE The opposite of contract is expand.

see also **expand**

contrast

Contrast means that there is a big difference between one object or one part of an object and another.

• The black and white diamond shapes create a **contrast** in this pattern.

control

❶ A control is a switch or device by which a machine or vehicle is regulated.

❷ A control is also part of an experiment which is kept the same in each test so that comparisons may be made.

controlled variable see variable

convection

When gases or liquids are heated they become lighter. This makes them rise and move. This movement is called convection.

• The **convection** of warm air round a room causes it to rise as it is heated and sink again as it cools.

see also **conduct, radiation**

a
b
c
d
e
f
g
h
i
j
k
l
m
n
o
p
q
r
s
t
u
v
w
x
y
z

convex

Convex means curved outwards, like the outside of a ball or circle. Mirrors or lenses that bulge out are convex. Convex mirrors give a wide angle of view.

• *A convex lens concentrates light.*

OPPOSITE The opposite of convex is concave.

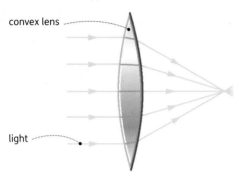

convex lens

light

see also **concave, lens, mirror, reflect**

cool

❶ Anything which is at a low temperature is said to be cool.

• *What might feel cool to one animal from the tropics might feel warm to an animal from the Arctic.*

❷ To cool something is to reduce its temperature.

see also **temperature**

copper

Copper is a reddish-brown metal. It is easy to bend and is a very good conductor of heat and electricity.

• *Electric wires are made of copper.*

copper wires

see also **conduct**

coral

A coral is a tiny animal that lives in tropical seas. Corals live in groups fixed to the sea bottom.

• *Many sea creatures live on coral reefs.*

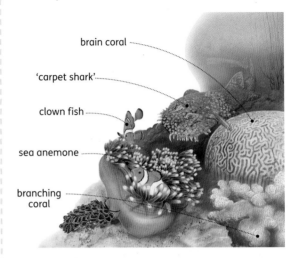

brain coral

'carpet shark'

clown fish

sea anemone

branching coral

cork

The bark of some oak trees is made of a thick layer of cork.

• *Large pieces of bark can be taken from cork trees without killing the tree.*

see also **bark**

cornea see eye

corrosion

Corrosion happens when chemicals cause a metal to be worn away.

• *Iron or steel rusting is one kind of* **corrosion**.

see also metal, rust

crab

A crab is an animal which lives in either salt or fresh water. It has a hard shell, a single pair of claws and eight legs.

• *There are many different types of* **crab**.

crab

cranium

The top part of the skull is called the cranium.

• *The brain is protected by the* **cranium**.

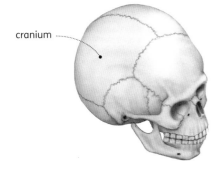

cranium

see also bone, brain, skull

crow

A crow is a large perching bird which is grey or black. Crows have thick bills and a loud call.

• *Crows are among the cleverest and most adaptable of birds.*

see also bill, bird

crustacean

A crustacean is an animal that usually has a hard shell and many legs. They are a type of arthropod. Most crustaceans live in the sea.

• *Crabs and shrimps are common* **crustaceans**.

see also arthropod, invertebrate

crystal

A crystal is a mineral with a regular shape and a glassy appearance.

• *The faces of a* **crystal** *are flat and reflect the light beautifully.*

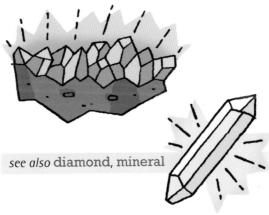

see also diamond, mineral

current

A flow of electricity is called a current. The units used to measure current are called amps.

• The **current** is the same at each point in a circuit.

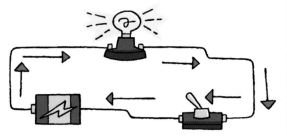

see also amp, battery, electricity

cutting

A cutting is a small part of a root or stem which can be grown into a new plant.

see also root, stem, plant

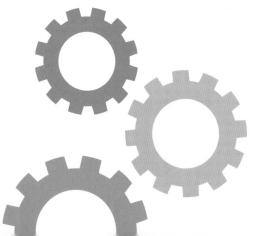

Dd

damage

When something is spoiled or harmed it is damaged. If you damage something, it will not work well and may be broken.

• Habitats and environments may be **damaged** by pollution or deforestation.

see also pollution, deforestation

dark

Dark means without light.

• The Earth rotates towards and away from the Sun. It is **dark** at night on the part of the Earth facing away from the Sun.

see also rotate, Sun, night

data

Data is information.

• *Data may be stored as numbers, symbols, pictures or text.*

WORD BUILD

➤ data logger

A data logger is a computer programme which uses sensors to record heat, light, motion or sound.

day

❶ A day lasts for 24 hours. This is the time it takes for the Earth to rotate once on its axis.

❷ Day also means the part of this time when it is light.

see also axis, night, rotate

dead

A living thing is dead if it cannot do the things that living things are able to do. Living things can move, reproduce, use their senses, grow, breathe, and feed.

• *A big tree may stay standing long after it is dead.*

see also alive, breathe, excrete, life, reproduction

decay

When a living thing dies bacteria and fungi make it decay. The chemicals released by decay are used by new living things.

see also bacterium, biodegradable, chemical, decompose, fungus, life

deciduous

Trees that lose their leaves once each year are deciduous.

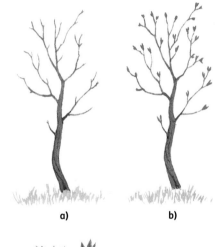

a)   b)

c)   d)

see also evergreen, leaf

a b c d e f g h i j k l m n o p q r s t u v w x y z

A B C D E F G H I J K L M N O P Q R S T U V W X Y Z

decompose

To decompose is to rot away. Dead plants and animal remains decompose to form new soil.

• *Some people use compost heaps to decompose waste in their garden to form new soil. Beetles, worms and other minibeasts help dead leaves to decompose.*

see also bacterium, compost, decay, fungus, rot

➤ **decomposition**

Decomposition is the process by which dead plant or animal remains are broken down into simple organic matter.

deforestation

Deforestation is the removal of trees from land which is then used for a non-forest purpose.

see also habitat, environment, damage

density

Materials with a high density are heavy for their size. Materials with a low density are light for their size.

• *Lead has a high density. It weighs much more than the same volume of polystyrene.*

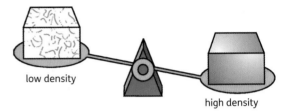

low density

high density

see also mass, volume, weight

dependent variable *see* variable

desert

A desert is a very dry place where it is hard for plants and animals to live. Deserts may be very hot near the equator or very cold near the poles.

see also cactus

42

development

Development is the change in a living organism or a community of living things.

➤ **develop**

To develop means to grow or to create something gradually.

device

A device is any mechanism which makes work easier.

see also mechanism, machine

dew

Dew drops form when water condenses out of the air. Dew covers plants on cool mornings.

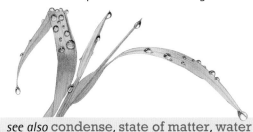

see also condense, state of matter, water

diabetes

Diabetes is a disease that stops people digesting sugar properly. A diabetic is a person with diabetes.

• *Diabetics don't have enough of a substance called insulin in their bodies. Many have to have regular injections of insulin.*

see also blood, digest, sugar

diagram

A diagram is a simplified drawing of information. Maps and illustrations are types of diagram.

• *The flow of electricity is easier to explain with a diagram.*

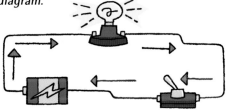

diamond

Diamond is a hard, clear type of crystal. It is made from carbon deep in the Earth's crust.

• *Diamonds are used in expensive jewellery.*

see also carbon, crystal, mineral

diarrhoea

Diarrhoea is runny faeces. It is often caused by bacteria in the intestines.

see also bacterium, faeces, intestine

a b c **d** e f g h i j k l m n o p q r s t u v w x y z

diet

Diet is the sort of food animals or people eat regularly.

see also food, health

difference

The difference between two objects or things is what helps us to tell them apart.

Spot the difference betwen both images above.
There are 3 differences.

digest

To digest is to break down food so that its nutrients can be absorbed by the body.

see also stomach, intestine

➤ digestive system

The digestive system is all the organs in the body that break down and digest food. They are linked by a tube from the mouth to the anus.

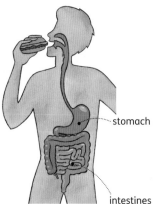

stomach

intestines

digital

Devices that use numbers to show or store information are digital. Computers store information in digital form. CDs store music in digital form.

• *Digital* watches do not have a dial.

dilute

To dilute a liquid is to make it become less concentrated. When a solution is diluted it is weaker.

OPPOSITE The opposite of dilute is concentrate.

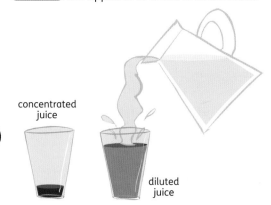

concentrated juice

diluted juice

see also concentrate, solution

dinosaur

Animals in the dinosaur group were reptiles which became extinct 65 million years ago.

• *Birds are related to the **dinosaurs**.*

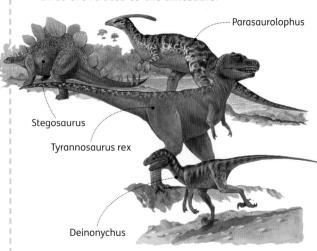

Parasaurolophus

Stegosaurus

Tyrannosaurus rex

Deinonychus

see also bird, extinct, reptile

disease

When a person is ill or sick, they may have a disease.

• *Arthritis is a **disease** that affects the joints.*

see also AIDS, cold, diabetes, joint

dispersal

Dispersal is the way something is spread out. Seeds and animals can disperse when they are ready to grow independently.

○ seed dispersal

Seed dispersal refers to the ways seeds are spread from the parent plant to a place they can grow.

• *Seed **dispersal** may be by wind, water or animals.*

displacement

Displacement is what happens when an object is placed in a container of liquid and it pushes some of the liquid out of the way. This causes the level of the liquid to rise. If you get into a bath completely full of water, some water will be displaced and spill out of the bath.

➤ displace

To displace is to move away.

see also float, upthrust

display

❶ To display is to show something.

• *Birds **display** to each other when they are ready to mate.*

❷ A display is a way of showing information.

• *A **display** after an experiment lets others know what has been done.*

dissolve

To dissolve in a liquid a solid mixes so completely with the liquid that it cannot be seen. This mixture of solid and liquid is called a solution.

• *Water with salt **dissolved** in it is clear like pure water, but you can taste the salt.*

see also liquid, saturated, solid, solute, solution

distance

Distance refers to how far away something is or how far an object has travelled. Distances may be measured in, for example, millimetres, kilometres or light years.

see also light year

a
b
c
d
e
f
g
h
i
j
k
l
m
n
o
p
q
r
s
t
u
v
w
x
y
z

distil

To distil water is one way to get rid of impurities in it. The liquid is heated. The vapour produced is then condensed (distilled). The condensed liquid is pure. The impurities are left behind.

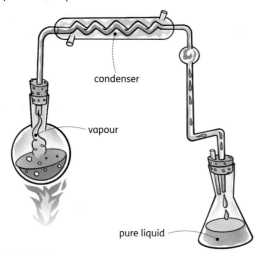

condenser

vapour

pure liquid

see also condense, evaporate, state of matter, vapour

DNA

DNA stands for *deoxyribonucleic acid.* DNA is a substance that contains all the information for our cells to reproduce correctly.

• *DNA is found in chromosomes inside our cells.*

see also cell, molecule, reproduction, chromosome

dormant

Something which is dormant appears to be dead or asleep.

• *A dormant volcano may erupt. A dormant animal may be hibernating. A dormant plant is not in a growing stage.*

see also stage, volcano, hibernate

drawing

A drawing is a graphical representation of an object or scene.

• *Drawings can be a useful way of recording data.*

see also data, diagram

drone

An unmanned aerial device which can be remotely controlled on its journeys is called a drone.

• *Drones can carry cameras.*

drug

A drug is a substance that has an effect in a person's body.

• *Many drugs are also medicines. They can be taken in many ways.*

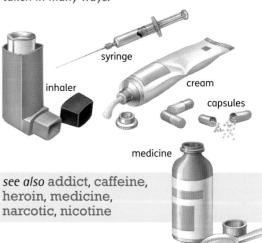

syringe

inhaler

cream

capsules

medicine

see also addict, caffeine, heroin, medicine, narcotic, nicotine

drunk

Someone is drunk when they have had too much alcohol and cannot control themselves.

see also alcohol, addiction

dwarf planet

A dwarf planet is an object which orbits a star, whose gravity is not strong enough to have attracted all the space debris near it.

• *Pluto is now seen as a **dwarf planet**.*

see also planet, gravity

Ee

ear

The ear is the organ with which we hear sound.

• *Animals such as rabbits have large external **ears** flaps to catch the faint sounds of hunting predators. Birds have all parts of their **ears** inside their heads.*

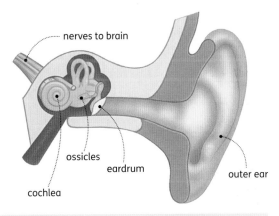

nerves to brain
ossicles
eardrum
outer ear
cochlea

see also organ, sound, vibration

Earth (*also* earth)

The planet on which we live is the Earth.

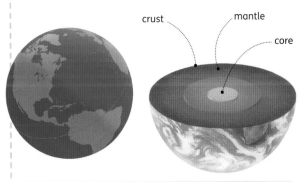

crust
mantle
core

see also atmosphere, Moon, planet

earthquake

An earthquake is the shaking of the surface of the Earth, caused by the movement of the rocks below.

• *Earthquakes can cause the ground to split.*

see also rock

earthworm

An earthworm is an invertebrate animal which lives in the soil.

see also invertebrate

echo

An echo is the repetition of sound caused by sound waves reflecting from a hard surface. There is a delay between the sound leaving the source and us hearing the echo. This is because sound takes time to travel.

• *You can hear an echo if a sound is made in a church or large cave.*

see also sound

eclipse

An eclipse happens when the Moon is directly in front of the Sun. It blocks the sunlight from reaching the Earth.

• *In a solar eclipse, the Sun's burning atmosphere (the corona) can be seen.*

see also lunar, Moon, Sun

ecology

Ecology is the study of living things and the way they live in their environment.

see also environment

ecosystem

An ecosystem includes the living things and non-living things in one place, and their relationship to each other.

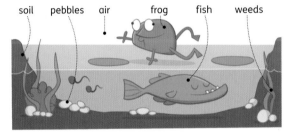

soil   pebbles   air   frog   fish   weeds

eczema

Eczema is a skin condition that causes the skin to be very dry and sore.

• *Eczema can be caused by an allergy to pets or to certain foods.*

see also allergy, disease

effect

An effect is the result of an action or a change of action.

egg

An egg is a roundish object that female animals produce. An egg can develop into a new baby animal if it is fertilised. In mammals, eggs grow inside the mother.

• *Birds' **eggs** have a hard shell. Reptiles' **eggs** are leathery.*

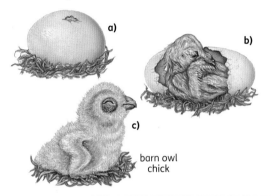

a)

b)

c)

barn owl chick

see also amphibian, bird, caterpillar, insect, ovum, reptile

elastic

Materials that are elastic spring back into their original shape after being stretched or compressed.

• *A spring is elastic.*

see also material

a
b
c
d
e
f
g
h
i
j
k
l
m
n
o
p
q
r
s
t
u
v
w
x
y
z

A B C D E F G H I J K L M N O P Q R S T U V W X Y Z

electric

A machine is electric if it is powered by electricity.

• *A computer is* **electric** *as it may be powered by mains electricity or* **electric** *cells.*

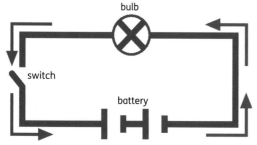

see also battery, cell

electrical cell see cell

electrical circuit see circuit

electrical insulation see insulation

electrical resistance see resistance

electricity

Electricity is a form of energy used for lighting, heating, making sound and making machines work.

• *In a lamp,* **electricity** *causes a wire in the bulb to glow and become hot.*

see also battery, bulb, cell, conduct, current, energy, work

electric symbols

Electric symbols represent the components in a circuit.

switch

battery

bulb

resistor

electron

An electron is part of an atom.

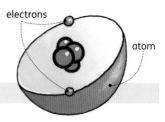
electrons
atom

see also atom

element

An element is the basic part of all materials. There are over 100 different elements. Elements combine to make compounds.

• *Pencil leads are made from the* **element** *carbon. Mercury is a liquid* **element** *used in thermometers. Oxygen gas is the* **element** *we need to breathe.*

see also atom, compound

embryo

❶ An animal embryo is the offspring of an animal before it is born or comes out of an egg.

• *A human* **embryo** *gets nourishment from its mother.*

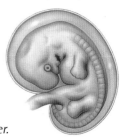

see also foetus, germinate, womb

❷ A plant embryo is a plant that is beginning to grow from a seed.

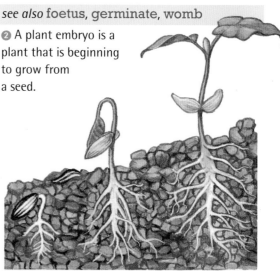

enamel

Enamel is the hard shiny covering layer on a tooth.

see also tooth

energy

Energy is what makes things move or get hot.

• *We mostly use* **energy** *in the form of electrical energy, heat or movement* **energy.**

see also calorie, kilojoule, work

⚙ renewable energy

Renewable energy supplies are those that will not run out. The wind, running water and the Sun can all be sources of renewable energy.

⚙ non-renewable energy

Forms of energy which cannot be renewed are called non-renewable. Fossil fuels such as coal and gas are non-renewable.

see also fossil fuel

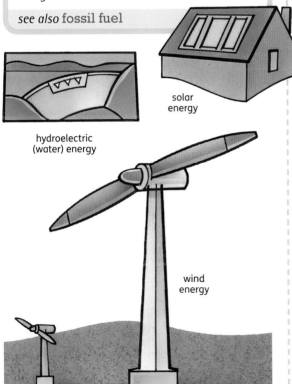

hydroelectric
(water) energy

solar
energy

wind
energy

enquiry

An enquiry may take place when there is something to find out.

➤ enquire

To enquire is to ask for information.

environment

The environment is the conditions in which a living thing exists. Soil, climate and other living things all count as part of the environment.

• *Rainforest plants need a wet* **environment.**

see also adapt, habitat

equator

The imaginary line around the Earth that is halfway between the North and South Poles is called the equator.

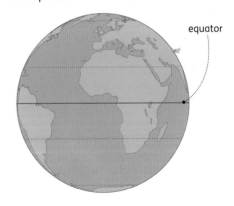

equator

see also pole

a
b
c
d
e
f
g
h
i
j
k
l
m
n
o
p
q
r
s
t
u
v
w
x
y
z

equinox

Equinox happens on the days that are halfway between midwinter and midsummer. On those days every place on Earth has 12 hours of daylight and 12 hours of night.

• *Equinoxes happen in autumn and spring.*

see *also* day, night, Sun

equipment

Equipment is what is needed for a particular purpose.

• *The equipment for a test includes items to help observe, measure and record the results.*

erosion

Water and wind wear away at rocks and soil. This process is called erosion.

see *also* rock

➤ **erode**

To erode is to wear away at rocks and soil over time.

• *Water and wind have eroded the rocks in Monument Valley, USA, into unusual shapes.*

evaporate

To evaporate is to change from a liquid to a gas

• *Water evaporates more quickly when it is warm and windy.*

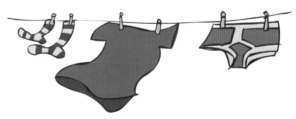

see *also* gas, liquid, state of matter, change of state

➤ **evaporation**

Evaporation is the change of state from a liquid to a gas.

evergreen

Trees and bushes that do not lose their leaves in winter are evergreen. Holly, pine trees and ivy are evergreen plants.

• *In tropical countries, where there is little difference between the seasons, many of the plants are* **evergreen**.

see *also* deciduous, leaf

evidence

Evidence is information which shows whether a test result is valid or not.

• **Evidence** *may be in the form of numbers, photos, reports or other data.*

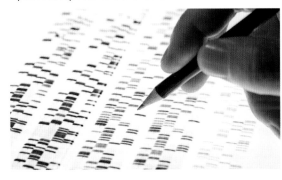

see *also* data, chart, graph

evolution

Evolution is the way in which plants and animals have changed over millions of years.

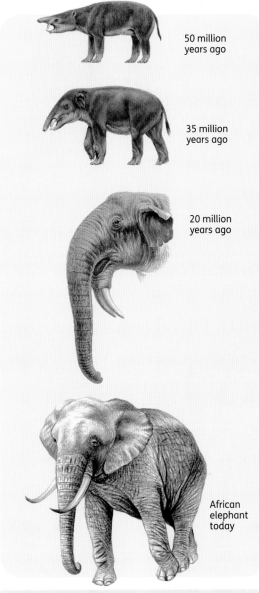

50 million years ago

35 million years ago

20 million years ago

African elephant today

see *also* bird, dinosaur, extinct, reptile

➤ evolve

Plants and animals evolve when they change over millions of years.

• *The earliest plants and animals were very simple. They have* **evolved** *into more complex ones over millions of years.*

excrete

Animals use their kidneys to filter waste from the blood. They excrete this in the form of urine. Solid waste is excreted as faeces.

see also faeces, urine, bladder

exercise

Exercise means using a lot of effort to move our bodies so that they stay fit and healthy.

• People can walk, dance, run or climb to keep fit. It can be fun to join a gym or an **exercise** class to keep fit.

☼ aerobic exercise

Aerobic exercise is exercise which makes you breathe deeply and increases your heart rate. It means there is a good supply of oxygen to the muscles.

expand

To expand is to become larger.

• Heat makes the mercury in a thermometer expand.

OPPOSITE The opposite of expand is contract.

see also contract

experiment

In an experiment you test an idea by changing one variable at a time to see what happens.

• In this **experiment** the student will find out how long the candle will burn in different-sized jars.

explain

To explain means to make things clear.

see also result, data, evidence

➤ explanation

An explanation should make results, evidence and data understandable. An explanation for why one car went faster than the other might say that one was pushed harder.

explode see explosion

explore

To explore is to find out how things work.

• *Ideas, places and habitats can be **explored**.*

see also investigate

➤ exploration

Exploration is the process of finding things out. A more organised way of doing this would be called an investigation.

explosion

An explosion is when a substance burns very rapidly. It gives a sudden burst of energy, often with a loud noise.

see also burn, energy

➤ explode

A substance explodes when it burns very rapidly and gives a sudden burst of energy. There may be a flash of light and a loud noise.

• *Fireworks are full of gunpowder, which **explodes** when they are set alight.*

extinct

Animals and plants that have died out completely are extinct.

• *Mammoths became **extinct** a few thousand years ago. Dodos became **extinct** more recently.*

passenger pigeon

moa

quagga

dodo

Tasmanian wolf

see also dinosaur, evolution, fossil

a
b
c
d
e
f
g
h
i
j
k
l
m
n
o
p
q
r
s
t
u
v
w
x
y
z

eye

The eye detects light. Light enters through the pupil. It passes through a lens which focuses light on the retina. Messages pass down the optic nerve.

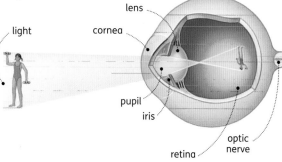

see also focus, lens

Ff

fabric

A fabric is a material which is woven, knitted or felted from textile threads such as wool or cotton.

see also material

WORD BUILD

➤ **cornea**

The cornea is the outer protective layer of the eye which appears white.
• *The **cornea** is a barrier against dirt and germs.*

➤ **iris**

The iris is the coloured part of the **eye** around the pupil.
• *In bright light the **iris** spreads out to make the pupil smaller. This protects the eye from the bright light.*

➤ **optic nerve**

The optic nerve carries information from the back of the eye to the brain.

➤ **pupil**

The hole in the centre of your eye is the pupil. Light goes into the eye through the pupil.

➤ **retina**

The retina is the part of the eye which detects light and colour.

factor

A factor is something that affects the results in an experiment.
• *Two **factors** which affect how well a plant grows are the amount of light and water that the plant gets.*

faeces

Animals make solid waste in the form of faeces.
• *The **faeces** of each mammal are quite different and can be used to identify the animal that has left them.*

see also excrete

fair test *see* test

familiar

Ideas or objects which are already known are familiar.

fat

People and many other animals have a layer of fat under their skin. This is a reserve for when food is scarce. Fat is found in foods like margarine and cheese and in some plant seeds.

• *Fat insulates an animal. Animals that live in very cold water need thick layers of fat to keep them warm.*

walrus

see also **food, insulate, skin**

feather

A feather is a soft light growth on the body of a bird. Only birds have feathers. Feathers keep birds warm by insulating their skin.

• *Wing feathers are strong, light and waterproof.*

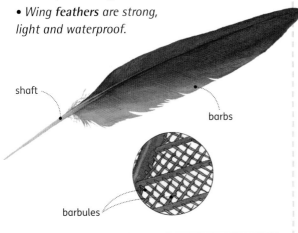

shaft

barbs

barbules

see also **bird, insulate, warm-blooded**

feature

An easily observed characteristic of something is a feature of it.

• *The features of a rock may be its colour, its hardness and its shape.*

female

The female of a species is the sex that makes eggs or seeds. Female animals usually look after the young.

see also **egg, flower, seed, species, male**

ferment

When sugar or carbohydrates ferment they are changed into alcohol and carbon dioxide. Yeast is a fungus that is used to ferment sugar in bread, beer, and wine.

• *Yeast ferments the flour and produces bubbles of carbon dioxide. These bubbles are trapped in the dough and make the bread light.*

see also **alcohol, carbohydrate, carbon dioxide, sugar**

a
b
c
d
e
f
g
h
i
j
k
l
m
n
o
p
q
r
s
t
u
v
w
x
y
z

fern

Ferns are a group of plants which reproduce with spores and not flowers and seeds. They often have divided leaves called fronds.

• *The spores can often be seen on the backs of the fern leaves.*

see also plant, non-flowering plant

fertilise (*also* fertilize)

To fertilise is to cause an egg or female plant to develop a new offspring. This happens when the male sperm reaches the female egg and fertilises it. The same thing happens in plants when the male pollen reaches the female ovule.

• *Usually only one male sperm will actually fertilise the female egg. Only a fertilised egg can develop into young.*

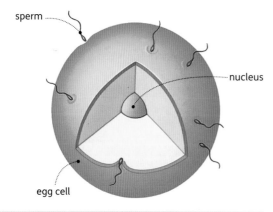

sperm

nucleus

egg cell

see also female, flower, male, ovary, pollen, sperm, ovule

➤ fertiliser

Fertiliser is a substance added to soil to make it better for growing plants.

• *Fertilisers may be made from natural compost or manufactured chemicals.*

fetus *see* foetus

fibre

Fibre is part of a healthy diet. It passes through the intestines unchanged. It can stop people being constipated.

• *Fruit, vegetables and wholemeal flour have lots of fibre.*

see also constipation, diet, faeces

fibula *see* bone

filter

❶ A filter is a device used to remove small particles or other solids from a liquid. Filters cannot separate solids that are in solution.

• *A filter can be made of paper, charcoal or any material with tiny holes in it. Here the solid materials are caught in the filter but the coffee solution passes through.*

filter

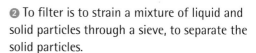

see also solution, separate

❷ To filter is to strain a mixture of liquid and solid particles through a sieve, to separate the solid particles.

➤ filtration

Filtration is the process of filtering something.

fire

Fire is burning gas. Wood and coal appear to burn, but it is really the gas coming from them as they are heated which is burning.

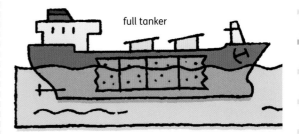

• *To get a fire going you need fuel, air and heat. To put it out you must cool it, starve it of air or remove the fuel.*

see also air, flame, fuel

fish

A fish is an animal with a backbone that has scales covering its body. It lives in water and breathes through gills.

• *Fish have backbones like all vertebrates.*

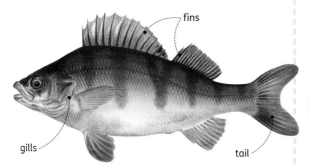

fins

gills

tail

see also gill, scale, vertebrate

flame

A flame is produced when something burns.

• *Solids and liquids do not burn directly. They have to produce a gas, and it is this that burns with a flame.*

see also burn, fire, gas

float

When an object floats it is being supported by water or air. The force that makes objects float is called upthrust.

• *A full tanker floats lower in the water than an empty one.*

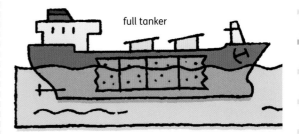

full tanker

empty tanker

see also hot-air balloon, submarine, upthrust, displacement

flower

A flower is the part of a plant that makes it able to reproduce. Once it has been fertilised, the flower produces fruit and seeds. The male anthers produce pollen. The pollen fertilises the female ovule.

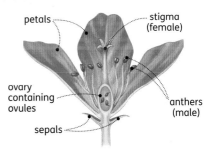

petals

stigma (female)

ovary containing ovules

anthers (male)

sepals

see also anther, female, fertilise, male, ovule, pollen, sexual reproduction

flowering plant *see* plant

flu *see* influenza

fluid
A fluid is a gas or liquid that moves freely.
• *Milk and oil are **fluids**.*

see also gas, liquid

focus
For an eye to focus it must adapt to the light available to make it possible to see clearly. When light is focused it makes a clear image. The lens in a camera focuses the image on the film or sensor.
• *The lenses in a telescope **focus** light from distant objects onto the eye.*

lens

lens

see also image, lens, light

foetus (*also* fetus)
An unborn baby that has been in the womb for more than eight weeks is called a foetus. Before that time it is known as an embryo.
• *A human **foetus** needs to stay inside the mother for about 9 months until it is ready to live on its own.*

see also embryo, womb

fog
Fog is made from tiny droplets of liquid water.

see also cloud, condense

foil
A very thin, flexible sheet of a metal such as aluminium is called a foil.
• *Aluminium **foil** is often used to protect food.*

food
Food gives living things energy. Animals need to eat plants or other animals for food. Plants make their own food from air, water and sunlight.

see also diet, energy, photosynthesis, health

➤ food chain

Animals eat plants or other animals. The way this happens is shown in a food chain.

➤ food group

Food can be divided into different food groups which maintain the body and are used by the body in different ways. Proteins are body building, fats keep us warm and carbohydrates give us energy.

see also protein, carbohydrate, fat, vitamin, fibre

➤ food pyramid

A food pyramid is a diagram which illustrates the plants and animals in an ecosystem which rely on each other for food.

see also ecosystem

➤ food web

A food web shows the way that food chains are linked.

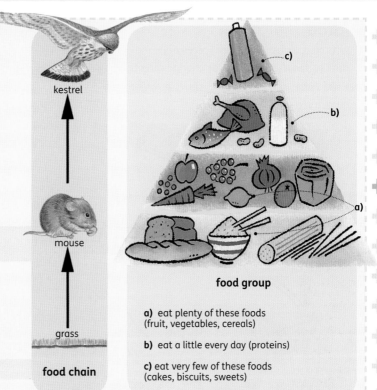

kestrel

mouse

grass

food chain

food group

a) eat plenty of these foods (fruit, vegetables, cereals)

b) eat a little every day (proteins)

c) eat very few of these foods (cakes, biscuits, sweets)

food web

killer whale

right whale

sperm whale

leopard seal

albatross

walrus

crabeater seal

penguin

fish

squid

krill

tiny plants

tiny animals

force

A force is a push or a pull. Forces make objects start to move, slow down or change direction.

• The **force** of air resistance slows a falling parachute.

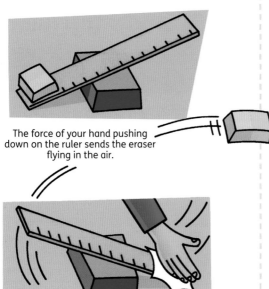

The force of your hand pushing down on the ruler sends the eraser flying in the air.

see also magnet, accelerate, air resistance, friction, gravity

formation

A group of animals, plants or objects in a particular pattern is a formation.

• Cell **formation** in a beehive involves tessellating hexagons.

fossil

The bones or other remains of living things are sometimes preserved in rocks as a fossil.

• **Fossils** can be millions of years old. They tell us about life in the past.

trilobite

see also ammonite, dinosaur, extinct, rock

fossil fuel see fuel

fracking

Fracking is a process where water containing sand and chemicals is injected into rocks containing natural gas or oil. This forces the oil or gas into a well from which it can be pumped.

see also natural gas, rock, oil

freeze

To freeze is for a liquid to become cold enough to turn into a solid. Chocolate freezes at room temperature, while water freezes at 0°C.

• Orange juice can be **frozen** to make lollies.

see also solid, liquid, Celsius, state of matter

freezing point

Freezing point is the temperature at which a liquid turns into a solid.

• The **freezing point** of water is 0° Celsius.
The **freezing point** of wax is room temperature.

see also Celsius, boiling point, liquid, solid

freshwater

Freshwater describes water that does not contain dissolved salt.

• *Most lake and river water is **freshwater** but 99% of the water on Earth is salty.*

see also **salt, water**

friction

When one surface moves against another, the rubbing force that tries to stop the movement is called friction. Friction slows all moving objects and gives off heat.

• ***Friction** helps tyres grip the road. **Friction** stops you when you put the brakes on.*

see also **force**

frog

A frog is an amphibian. It is a vertebrate which lays its eggs in water.

• *Tadpoles hatch from eggs, and develop into adult **frogs** which live on land.*

see also **development, amphibian, hatch**

frost

Frost is frozen condensation. It happens when the air temperature is below 0°C. Ground frost happens when the ground is colder than the air.

• *When it is really cold, **frost** can turn the trees white.*

see also condense, freeze

fruit

The fruit of a plant is formed from its ovary. It protects the seeds. Animals are attracted to eat the fruit and spread the seed.

orange

pea

strawberry

maple tree

see also flower, ovary, ovule, seed

fuel

Fuel is a substance that can be burned to give heat or light. Most fuels contain carbon compounds.

• *Fuels may be solid, liquid or gas.*

petrol

wood

see also burn, carbon, compound, energy

○ fossil fuels

Coal, oil and gas are all types of fossil fuel. They were formed millions of years ago. Once they are used up they are not renewed.

• *At the moment we depend for most of our energy on burning **fossil fuels**.*

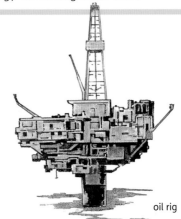

oil rig

coal-fired power staion

function

The task that something has is its function.
The reason for something to exist is its function.
The use of something is its function.

• *The **function** of a data logger is to collect data. The **function** of an eye is to enable an animal to see.*

fungus (*plural* fungi)

A fungus looks like a plant, but it does not contain chlorophyll. Fungi are a group of living things that are neither plants nor animals. Some fungi are poisonous.

• ***Fungi** cannot make their own food and so have to live on other dead or living organisms.*

shaggy ink cap

mushroom

bracket fungus

see also chlorophyll, mushroom, plant, rot, yeast

fuse

A fuse is an electrical device that contains a thin piece of wire. The wire melts if the electric current going through it gets too big.

• ***Fuses** are a safety feature of all plugs and most electrical appliances.*

fuse

see also current, electricity

Gg

galaxy

A galaxy is an enormous group of stars. There may be billions of stars in a single galaxy.

• *Our solar system is in a **galaxy** we call the Milky Way.*

garden

A garden is an area of land, where the grass, plants and features such as paths are arranged by people. A garden may contain a wildlife area.

• *Some people grow fruit and vegetables as well as flowers in their **garden**.*

gas

A gas is a substance with no fixed shape or volume. Most gases are invisible, but some smell strongly, for example chlorine.

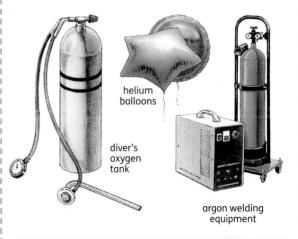

helium balloons

diver's oxygen tank

argon welding equipment

see also volume, natural gas, hydrogen, oxygen, nitrogen

a b c d e f g h i j k l m n o p q r s t u v w x y z

gastropod

A gastropod is an animal that moves around on a single fleshy foot. The name means 'stomach foot'. Gastropods are molluscs.

• Snails are **gastropods**.

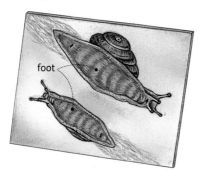

see also invertebrate, mollusc

gather

To gather is to collect. Evidence needs gathering to find the result of a test.

gauge

A gauge is a standard measuring scale. The word gauge rhymes with 'cage'.

gear

A gear is a toothed wheel. Two gears meshed together can alter the speed and direction of a turning movement.

gender

A living thing is usually either male or female gender. Some animals are hermaphrodites.

• *Living things of both **genders** are usually needed to reproduce. Exceptions are some small animals such as aphids.*

see also female, hermaphrodite, male

gene

A gene is a short length of chromosome. Genes are responsible for eye colour, hair colour, blood type and inherited disease.

• *People pass on their **genes** when they reproduce.*

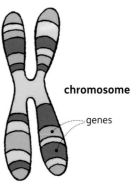

chromosome

genes

see also chromosome, DNA, reproduction

generator

A generator is a device that produces electricity.

• *Turning the blades of the turbine on a **generator** turns a coil of wire between two magnets. This produces electricity.*

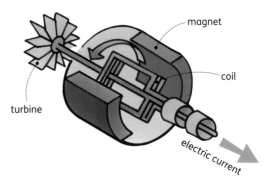

magnet

coil

turbine

electric current

genitals

The word genitals refers to the external sexual organs of animals.

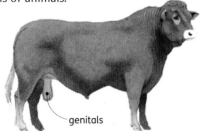

genitals

see also penis, sexual intercourse, testicle, vagina

geocentric

Geocentric refers to the Earth being the centre of the universe. It is not the centre of the universe.

see also heliocentric

geology

Geology is the study of rocks.

see also rock

➤ geologist

A geologist is a person who studies geology.

germ

A germ is a micro-organism that can infect us and cause disease.

see also bacterium, fungus, micro-organism, virus

germinate

When a seed sprouts, it germinates. A seed needs warmth and water to germinate. Light is not needed to make most seeds start growing.

see also seed

gestation

Gestation is the period that a foetus stays in its mother's body. This word applies only to mammals.

• *Different mammals have different **gestation** periods.*

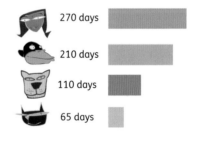

270 days

210 days

110 days

65 days

see also foetus, mammal

gill

A gill is what allows animals that live in water to breathe.

• ***Gill** flaps cover a fish's **gills**.*

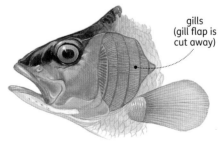

gills (gill flap is cut away)

see also fish

glass

Glass is a hard, shiny, brittle material that is usually transparent. It is made by melting sand with other chemicals.

• *Glassblowers blow hot **glass** into shapes such as bottles and vases.*

see also brittle, chemical, transparent

global warming

Global warming is the term used to describe the rising temperature of the Earth's climate. Scientists think it is happening because we burn fuel. The gases produced cause a greenhouse effect.

• *As a result of **global warming**, as the Earth warms up, the ice at the North and South Poles begins to melt and break up.*

see also burn, carbon dioxide, fossil fuel, gas, greenhouse effect

GM

GM is short for *genetically modified*. This means changing the genes in the cells of a living thing. Scientists have developed GM food plants that grow bigger or resist disease.

• *Some people think **GM** crops will be very useful. Others think they are dangerous.*

gold

Gold is a yellow metal that is soft and easily shaped. It is a very dense material.

• ***Gold** does not lose its shiny colour so has been used as a precious metal throughout human history.*

see also density, material, metal

grain

Grain is the seeds of wheat and other cereals.

• *People eat many types of **grain**.*

see also cereal

granite *see* rock

graph

A graph is a diagram that helps show information.

• The bar **graph** shows favourite foods in our class.

see also **chart**

○ bar graph

A bar graph shows the data in bars. They may be horizontal or vertical.

○ line graph

A line graph shows the data as a line joining a series of points. Line graphs are often used to show temperatures.

favourite foods in a class

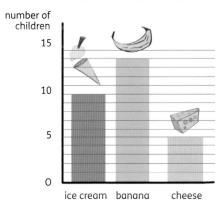

bar graph

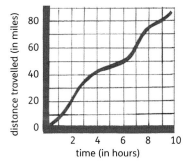

line graph

graphite

Pencil leads are made from graphite. It is a form of carbon.

see also **carbon, lead**

grass

Grass is a flowering plant with long thin leaves. Bamboo, wheat, maize and oats are all types of grass.

• All **grasses** are pollinated by the wind.

see also **cereal, flower, pollinate**

gravity

The force that attracts objects to the Earth is called gravity.

• When an apple falls from a tree it is pulled down by **gravity**.

see also **Earth, force**

greenhouse effect

The way that the Earth's atmosphere traps heat from the Sun is called the greenhouse effect. Some heat is absorbed by gases in the atmosphere.

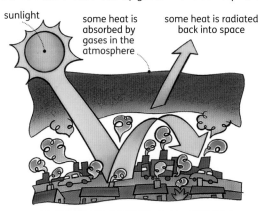

sunlight

some heat is absorbed by gases in the atmosphere

some heat is radiated back into space

see also **atmosphere, ozone**

a b c d e f g h i j k l m n o p q r s t u v w x y z

greenhouse gases

Greenhouse gases are those which contribute to global warming. These gases are carbon dioxide, methane and polluting gases from burning fossil fuels.

see also fossil fuel, pollution

group

To group things is to put them into different categories.

• Recycling involves **grouping** metal, plastic and glass waste into different bins.

grow

To grow is to get bigger in size. All living things grow for part of their lives.

• Young plants and animals **grow** faster than older ones.

grub

Grub is another word for the larva of an insect.

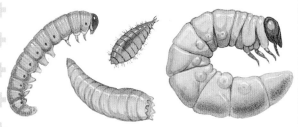

see also insect, larva

gums

The gums are the part of the mouth in which our teeth are fixed.

see also tooth

gut

The gut is another word for the intestines.

• In the past, pigs' **guts** were used to make sausage skins.

Hh

habitat

A habitat is where a group of plants and animals live.

• A **habitat** might be one field or area of woodland. Desert and mountain **habitats** have very different plants and animals.

see also adapt, environment

○ micro-habitat

A micro-habitat is a very small habitat. It might be just under one tree or log or a single rock pool.

hard

A material or object which is hard is tough, rigid and not easily broken or bent.

• **Hard** materials are solid and firm such as rock or brick.

hatch

To hatch means to emerge from an egg.

head

The head of an animal is the part which contains the brain, mouth, eyes and other sensing organs.

health

The health of a plant or animal is how well or ill it is.

• *Good health means being free from illness or injury.*

➤ **healthy diet**

A healthy diet is one which keeps a person or animal well and not overweight.

• *A healthy diet for people is one which has a balance of foods from all food groups.*

see also diet

➤ **healthy food**

Healthy food has the nutrients in it which the body needs.

a) eat plenty of these foods (fruit, vegetables, cereals)

b) eat a little every day (proteins)

c) eat very few of these foods (cakes, biscuits, sweets)

see also food

heart

The heart is a pump that pushes blood round the body.

see also artery, blood, capillary, vein

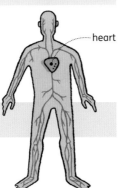

heart

heat

metal spoon

❶ Heat is a form of energy. It can be measured using a thermometer.

• *Heat travels easily through metals.*

❷ To heat an object is to raise its temperature and make it warmer.

see also conduct, energy, temperature, thermal, thermometer

heat insulation *see* insulation

heliocentric

All the planets in the solar system orbit the Sun. This means that their orbit is heliocentric.

see also solar, geocentric, orbit

helium

Helium is the second lightest gas in the universe. We use it to make balloons float at birthday parties.

see also gas

herbivore

An animal that only eats plants is a herbivore. Herbivores are the second link in many food chains.

• *Deer are herbivores.*

see also carnivore, omnivore, food chain

heredity

Heredity is the process that makes living things grow to look like their parents. People inherit the way they look from their mother and father.

see also chromosome, gene, inheritance

hermaphrodite

A living thing that has both male and female sex organs is a hermaphrodite.

• Earthworms are **hermaphrodites** but they cannot fertilise their own eggs. They give sperm to each other when they mate.

see also egg, fertilise, genitals, sperm

heroin

Heroin is a dangerous drug made from a type of poppy.

• Some **heroin** users inject. Others smoke it.

see also addict, drug, narcotic

hibernate

To hibernate an animal hides from the world and goes to sleep, usually in winter when food is scarce.

• Bears and butterflies **hibernate** in winter.

Homo sapiens

All people alive today are members of the species Homo sapiens.

see also species

honey

Bees make honey from the nectar they collect from flowers. Bees feed honey to their growing larvae.

• Bees store **honey** in a honeycomb.

see also flower, larva, nectar

horseshoe magnet
see magnet

hot-air balloon

A hot-air balloon has a gas heater to warm the air in the bag. This makes the air inside the bag lighter. Upthrust from the air makes the balloon rise. The hot air in the balloon is less dense than the cooler surrounding air.

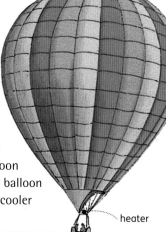

heater

see also air, gas, gravity, upthrust

young adults   teenager   child   toddler   baby

human (*also* human being)

Human beings are people. You are a human being.

humerus *see* bone

humus

Humus is plant remains that have rotted away and mixed with the top part of the soil.

• *Humus* enriches the soil.

much humus

less humus

rock

see *also* decay, rot, soil

hurricane

A hurricane is a huge mass of spinning rain and wind. Storms like this are called typhoons when they occur over the Pacific Ocean.

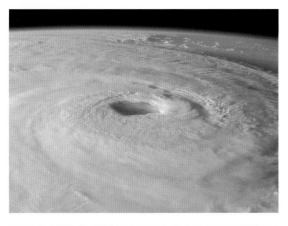

see *also* typhoon

hydrogen

Hydrogen is a gas that burns very easily. Water is made by burning hydrogen. It is the lightest gas.

• *Hydrogen* is used as a fuel in rockets.

see *also* gas, water

hygiene

Hygiene means keeping where you live clean and free from germs.

a
b
c
d
e
f
g
h
i
j
k
l
m
n
o
p
q
r
s
t
u
v
w
x
y
z

ice

Ice is the solid form of water. Ice forms when water freezes.

see also **water, freeze**

identify

To identify something is to be able to name it correctly. To accurately identify an object you have to know exactly what it looks like.

• *It is useful to be able to **identify** the difference between a harmless hover fly and a wasp with a sting.*

wasp

hover fly

➤ identification

Identification is the skill of knowing what type of living thing, object or material something is.

igneous rock *see* rock

image

An image is a picture formed by a lens in a camera.

• *The photographer has taken an **image** of the Eiffel Tower.*

see also **lens, light**

immune system

The immune system produces chemicals that attack dangerous viruses and stop them from harming the body.

see also **vaccinate**

immunise (*also* immunize, inoculate, vaccinate)

To immunise people or animals is to inject them with dead germs. This helps the body protect itself against a real virus or bacteria attack.

see also **bacterium, germ, virus**

impermeable

An impermeable substance is one that liquids and gases cannot pass through.

• *Water cannot go through* **impermeable** *materials.*

OPPOSITE The opposite of impermeable is permeable.

see also permeable, water

incisor *see* tooth

incubate

When birds incubate their eggs, they sit on them to keep them warm until their chicks hatch.

see also egg

➤ incubation

Birds start to develop in the egg, which provides the right conditions for development. This is called incubation.

➤ incubator

An incubator is a machine which keeps living things at the best temperature for their development. Micro-organisms grow faster if they are kept warm in an incubator.

• *Some tiny babies need to be kept warm in an* **incubator.**

independent variable
see variable

indigenous

If a plant or animal is indigenous to a place, it lives naturally there.

• *The kangaroo is* **indigenous** *to Australia.*

OPPOSITE The opposite of indigenous is alien.

see also alien

infect

Germs infect a person when they get inside their body. Once they are there they can multiply.

see also germ, virus

➤ infection

An infection occurs when the body is invaded by germs or viruses.

• *Germs may cause* **infection** *in a cut.*
The common cold is caused by a viral **infection.**

inflammable

Inflammable materials burn very easily. Hydrogen is a highly inflammable gas.

• *Candles are made from* **inflammable** *wax.*

see also flame, gas, hydrogen, solid

influenza (*also* flu)

Influenza is an infection caused by a virus. It is known as flu for short.

• *It is important to rest and drink lots of fluids when you have the **flu**.*

see also immunise, virus

infra-red

Infra-red is energy which we feel as heat.

• *The television remote control works using **infra-red**.*

inheritance

Inheritance is the physical features that are passed from parent to offspring. For example, hair and eye colour are features passed from parent to child.

inoculate *see* immunise

inorganic

Inorganic things do not come from living organisms. Rocks and metal are inorganic.

• *Nylon is **inorganic**.*

OPPOSITE The opposite of inorganic is organic.

see also nylon, organic

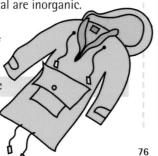

insect

An insect is an animal that has three parts to its body and six legs.

• *Most **insects** have wings, but only wasps, bees, hornets and some ants have a sting.*

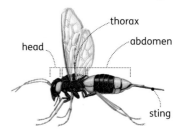

head · thorax · abdomen · sting

see also abdomen, beetle, thorax

insoluble

Solids that do not dissolve in a liquid are insoluble.

• *Flour is **insoluble** in water.*

OPPOSITE The opposite of insoluble is soluble.

see also liquid, solid, soluble, solute, solution, solvent

instinct

Animals know how to do some things by instinct. They do not have to be taught.

• *These baby turtles act on **instinct** when they run towards the sea.*

insulate

① To insulate for heat means to slow down the movement of heat through a material.

see also **conduct**

② To insulate for electricity means to stop electricity passing through.

➤ insulator

An electrical insulator does not allow electricity to pass through it.

• *The plastic around the wire is a good **insulator**. It protects people from getting electric shocks.*

A heat insulator does not allow heat to pass through it.

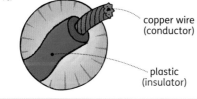

copper wire (conductor)

plastic (insulator)

see also **fat, feather**

③ A sound insulator does not allow sound to pass through it.

insulation

Insulation is done by putting a material between the source of energy and elsewhere.

➤ electrical insulation

Electrical insulation is provided by materials such as wood which do not conduct electricity.

➤ heat insulation

Materials that provide heat insulation stop heat from travelling to a cooler place.

• *Oven gloves act as **insulation** to keep the heat from the oven burning the man's hands.*

➤ sound insulation

Sound insulation muffles loud noises. Soft woolly materials or polystyrene can do this.

insulator *see* **insulate**

intestine

After food has been in the stomach it passes through the intestine. This is where most digestion happens.

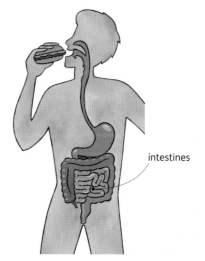

intestines

see also **digest, gut, stomach**

invent

To invent means to design or make something new.

➤ invention

An invention is a new object or system created by someone.

➤ inventor

An inventor is a person who comes up with new ideas for making objects and systems.

• *Alexander Graham Bell was the **inventor** of the telephone.*

• *Maria Beasley was the **inventor** of the life raft which saves lives at sea.*

a
b
c
d
e
f
g
h
i
j
k
l
m
n
o
p
q
r
s
t
u
v
w
x
y
z

invertebrate

Animals that do not have backbones are invertebrates.

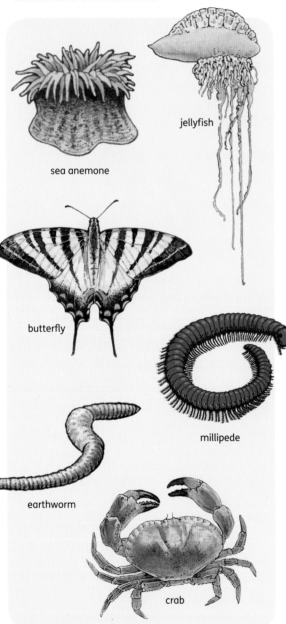

sea anemone

jellyfish

butterfly

millipede

earthworm

crab

see also insect, spine, vertebrate

investigate

When scientists investigate they are trying to find out what happens when something is changed.

• *These children are **investigating** what happens if you change the size of a parachute.*

see also experiment

➤ **investigation**

An investigation is an enquiry into something which is not known.

• *Scientists discover new facts about the world. Rosalind Franklin made **investigations** into DNA and found out how it worked.*

iris *see* eye

iron

Iron is a metal. It is very strong. When small amounts of carbon and other metals are added iron becomes steel.

• *Iron ore is the type of rock we get **iron** from. We get **iron** by heating **iron** ore in a blast furnace.*

iron ore, the type of rock we get iron from

blast furnace

see also carbon, rust, steel

irreversible change *see* change

Jj

Kk

joint

The place where two bones meet is a joint.

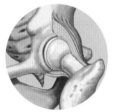

ball-and-socket
or swivel joint (hip)

hinge joint (knee)

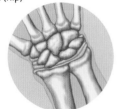

sliding joint (wrist)

see also bone

joule

The joule is a unit of measurement for work or energy. J is the abbreviation of joules.

⚙ kilojoule

The kilojoule is a unit of measurement for work or energy. The amount of food energy is measured in kilojoules. There are 1000 joules in a kilojoule. The abbreviation of kilojoule is kJ.

• *10-year-old children need approximately 10,000 kilojoules of food energy each day.*

see also calorie, energy, food, work

kidney

A kidney is an organ which filters the blood. Kidneys remove unwanted chemicals. These are diluted with water to make urine.

• *Mammals have two kidneys.*

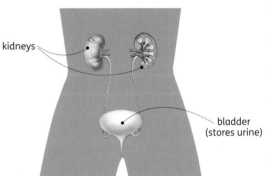

kidneys

bladder
(stores urine)

see also dilute, excrete, urine, bladder, chemical

kilogram

The kilogram is the unit we use to measure mass.

• *One litre of water has a mass of one kilogram.*

1
kg

1
litre

see also mass

kilojoule *see* joule

a
b
c
d
e
f
g
h
i
j
k
l
m
n
o
p
q
r
s
t
u
v
w
x
y
z

kinetic energy

Kinetic energy is another word for movement energy. Light objects moving slowly have very little kinetic energy. Heavy, fast moving objects have lots.

• A cyclist has lots of **kinetic energy**. A parked car has no **kinetic energy**.

see also energy

label

A label is a sign which gives information about the object or material it is with.

• *A label may be part of a diagram or put beside an object on a display.*

laboratory

The place where people conduct tests, experiments and investigations is a laboratory

• *Scientists and inventors work in a **laboratory**. Hospitals and schools have **laboratories** where people perform tests.*

larva (*plural* larvae)

A larva is in the caterpillar stage of an insect. Larvae of flies are called maggots.

• *Insect eggs hatch into **larvae**. **Larvae** form pupae. Pupae form into adults.*

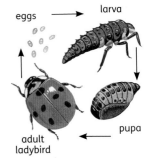

see also caterpillar, insect, life cycle, maggot, pupa

laser

A laser produces a very concentrated light beam. Some are used in delicate surgery on eyes. Powerful lasers can even cut through metal.

- *CD players use **lasers** to read CDs.*

lava

Lava is liquid rock that comes from a volcano. As a liquid it is very hot. Lava can travel a long way from the volcano before it cools and becomes hard rock.

- ***Lava** from volcanoes in Italy have destroyed farms and cities.*

lead

❶ Lead is a soft, dense, grey metal. It makes marks on paper.

- ***Lead** was once used for water pipes and added to petrol. This has stopped because **lead** is very poisonous.*

see also **density, metal**

❷ Pencil lead is made from a mixture of graphite (a form of carbon) and dry clay.

see also **carbon, clay, graphite**

leaf (*plural* leaves)

A leaf is the part of a plant where the plants makes its food using the process of photosynthesis.

- *We eat some kinds of **leaves**.*

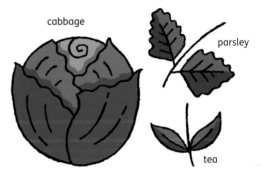

cabbage

parsley

tea

see also **food, photosynthesis**

lens

A lens is a piece of glass or plastic with two curved surfaces. Lenses are used in microscopes, telescopes and cameras.

see also **concave, convex, image, light**

lever

A lever is a long rod that pivots. A small force on the long end of the rod makes a bigger force on the short end.

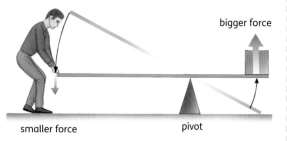

bigger force

smaller force · pivot

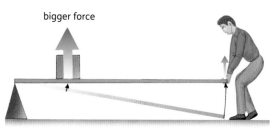

bigger force

smaller force

see also force, pivot

lice see louse

lichen

A lichen is a low crusty plant which grows on rocks, walls and trees. Lichens are very slow growing and most cannot live in polluted air.

• *Lichen reproduce with spores.*

life

Life is what separates living things from objects and materials which are not alive.

• *Plants and animals have **life**. We know they are alive when they feed, excrete, breathe, move, reproduce and are sensitive to the world around them.*

➤ life cycle

A life cycle shows the way in which a living thing changes as it grows. It also describes the way in which reproduction takes place.

• *Insects have one of two types of **life cycle**.*

see also insect, larva, reproduction

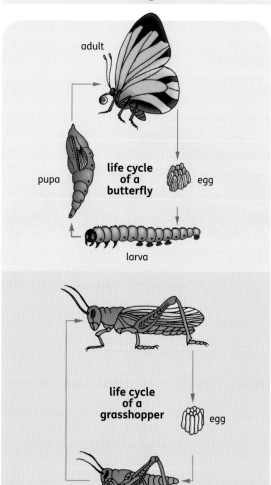

adult

pupa

life cycle of a butterfly

egg

larva

life cycle of a grasshopper

egg

nymph

➤ life processes

The life processes common to all living things are the ability to feed, excrete, breathe, move, reproduce and show awareness of world around them.

see also **carbon dioxide, environment, excrete, food, gas, oxygen, reproduction**

lifestyle

Lifestyle refers to how people choose to live.

• *Some people choose a vegetarian **lifestyle** by not eating meat or fish.*

see also **vegetarian**

light

Light is a form of energy we can detect with our eyes. Light can be split into the colours of the spectrum.

• *Where an object blocks the **light**, you get a shadow.*

see also **colour, energy, rainbow, spectrum, prism**

➤ light source

A light source may be natural such as the Sun or Moon, or it may be an artificial one from lamps or torches.

lightning

Lightning is the flash of light caused when an electrical spark jumps between clouds. The spark can also jump between a cloud and the ground.

• *During thunderstorms, **lightning** can strike buildings, trees or animals.*

see also **electricity, thunder**

light source *see* light

light year

A light year is a measure of distance. It is the distance travelled by light in one year.

• *The distance to our nearest star (apart from the Sun) is over four **light years**.*

limb

A limb is a part of the body that sticks out. Legs, arms and wings are all limbs.

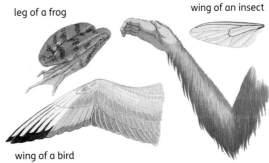

leg of a frog

wing of an insect

wing of a bird

arm of an ape

limestone *see* rock

line chart *see* chart

line graph *see* graph

liquid

A liquid can flow and take the shape of its container.

• *In a **liquid** the particles flow over each other.*

see also **fluid, gas, solid**

a
b
c
d
e
f
g
h
i
j
k
l
m
n
o
p
q
r
s
t
u
v
w
x
y
z

litter

Litter means any article or substance which is left or dumped in a place where it looks unsightly or might cause damage.

• *Litter such as plastic cups dumped on this beach can trap wildlife.*

liver

The liver is one of the main organs of the body. It is an energy store and the body's main producer of chemicals.

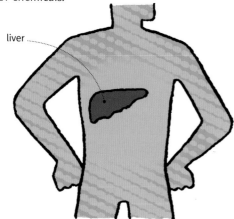

liver

see also chemical, energy, organ

living

Something which is living is alive and shows the characteristics of living things.

see also alive, life, dead

log

❶ When you log results you keep a record of them.

see also data

❷ A log is a record of something.

loud

The volume of a sound is loud when it has a lot of energy. A high volume gives a loud sound.

see also volume, energy

louse (*plural* lice)

Lice are the blood-sucking insects that sometimes live on people's skin.

• *You can tell a louse is an insect because it has six legs.*

lunar

Lunar means to do with the Moon.

• *In a lunar eclipse the position of the Earth stops the Sun's light from hitting the Moon.*

see also eclipse

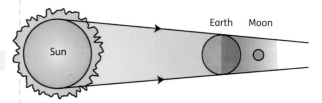

Sun   Earth   Moon

► lunar month

A lunar month is the time it takes for the Moon to orbit the Earth once. It is about 28 days.

see also Moon, orbit

lung

The lung is an organ that takes in oxygen from the air and excretes carbon dioxide from the body. Mammals have two lungs.

• *Not all animals have **lungs**. Insects and fish breathe in other ways.*

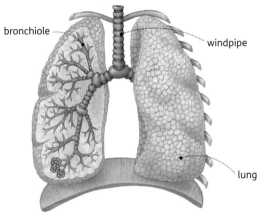

bronchiole

windpipe

lung

see also air, carbon dioxide, excrete, oxygen, gill

Mm

machine

Machines help us do work.

• *Cars are complicated **machines** with many different parts. They help us to move about quickly.*

see also gear, lever, work

maggot

A maggot is a larva. There are many types of maggot.

• *People often use **maggots** as bait when they are fishing with a rod and line.*

see also larva, pupa

a
b
c
d
e
f
g
h
i
j
k
l
m
n
o
p
q
r
s
t
u
v
w
x
y
z

A B C D E F G H I J K L **M** N O P Q R S T U V W X Y Z

magma

Magma is molten rock that is deep underground. It is called lava when it flows from a volcano.

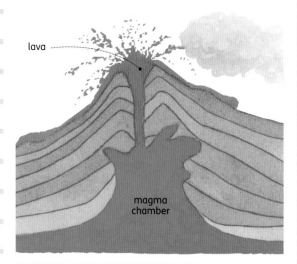

lava

magma chamber

see also rock, lava, volcano

magnet

A magnet is a piece of iron or steel that exerts a magnetic force.

see also magnetism

○ bar magnet

A bar magnet is a straight magnet with a north pole at one end and a south pole at the other end.

○ button magnet

A button magnet is round and in the shape of a button. The north and south poles are on the two flat sides. Magnets should include a metal keeper to help keep the magnet's strength.

○ horseshoe magnet

A horseshoe magnet is a bent magnet with a north pole on one branch and a south pole on the other branch.

magnetic pole

The magnetic poles on a magnet attract pieces of iron and steel. A north pole and a south pole attract each other. Two north poles, or two south poles, repel each other.

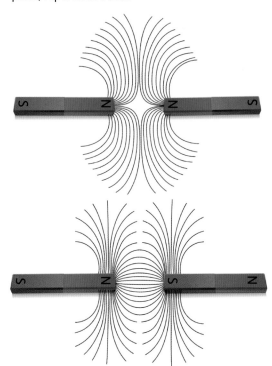

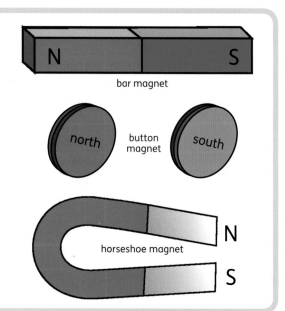

bar magnet

north   button magnet   south

horseshoe magnet

N

S

magnetism

Magnetism is an invisible force that attracts the metals iron, steel, cobalt and nickel.

• *Magnetism attracts iron filings and steel paperclips.*

see *also* force, iron, steel

magnify

To magnify is to make something appear larger.

• *A magnifying glass makes things look larger.*

see *also* lens, microscope

male

The male of an animal species is the sex that produces sperm. The male parts of a flower produce pollen.

see *also* anther, flower, semen, sperm, pollen, testicle, female

mammal

A mammal is a type of animal. A mammal's skin is usually hairy. They feed their young on milk and most give birth to live young.

• *Whales, humans, lions, bats and mice are some examples of mammals.*

chipmunk

orangutan

platypus

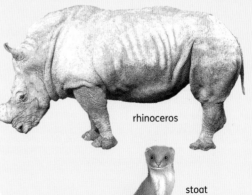

rhinoceros

stoat

see *also* animal

a
b
c
d
e
f
g
h
i
j
l
m
n
o
p
q
r
s
t
u
v
w
x
y
z

manufactured

Manufactured objects and materials are those made by people.

• *Many **manufactured** goods are made in factories.*

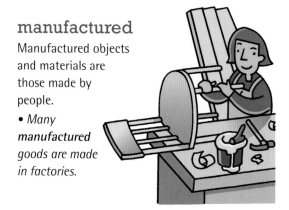

see also material, natural, plastic

mass

Mass is the amount of a substance. Mass is measured in grams and kilograms. Compare this with weight.

• *The **mass** of something does not change, wherever you measure it.*

see also density, kilogram, weight

material

A material is what an object is made from. It may be made from more than one type of substance.

• *The **material** used for a jersey may have cotton and wool in it.*

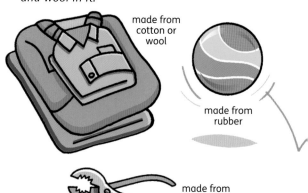

made from cotton or wool

made from rubber

made from steel

see also manufactured, natural, plastic, substance

matter

Matter is the scientific word for the stuff that all things are made of. The Sun, Moon, sand, air, plants and animals are all made of matter.

a sunflower

mature

Mature means to be fully developed or ripe.

• *It is best to eat fruit when it is **mature** and not unripe.*

maximum

The biggest amount is the maximum.

• *The **maximum** temperature ever recorded in Britain was 38.5°C.*

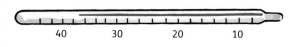

40 30 20 10

see also minimum

measles see childhood illness

measure

To measure is to find out the size of something using a calibrated measuring device.

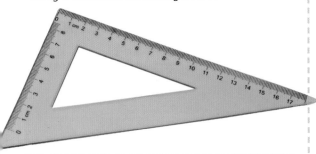

see also calibrate

mechanism

A mechanism is a system of moving parts working together. Several mechanisms working together create a machine.

see also machine

medicine

A medicine is a mixture of chemicals we take to make us feel better or to cure a disease.

• *Antibiotics are medicines that kill bacteria.*

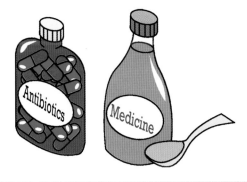

see also antibiotic, chemical, disease

medium

A medium is the stuff in which an organism lives. It may also be the material in which a plant is grown.

• *Some plants are grown in a medium which contains no soil.*

melt

To melt is to turn from a solid to a liquid.

• *Ice melts at room temperature.*

• *Chocolate melts in warm hands because they are at a higher temperature.*

• *A lolly left out of the freezer will melt.*

see also temperature

melting point

The melting point of a solid is the temperature at which it turns from a solid to a liquid.

• *The melting point for iron is much higher than the melting point for wax.*

menstruation

Women lose a small amount of blood each month through menstruation. The blood carries the unfertilised egg out of the womb and vagina.

• *Women use tampons or sanitary towels to soak up menstrual blood during times of menstruation.*

see also egg, period, vagina, womb

mercury

Mercury is a silvery metal. It is liquid at room temperature. Mercury is used in thermometers.

• *Mercury rises up a thermometer as it heats up and expands.*

see also liquid, thermometer

A B C D E F G H I J K L **M** N O P Q R S T U V W X Y Z

metal

A metal is a material that conducts electricity and heat. Gold, copper and iron are metals.

• The **metal** pins on a plug conduct electricity, while the plastic covering does not. A **metal** radiator conducts heat.

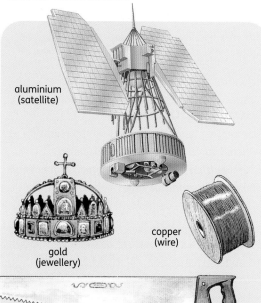

aluminium
(satellite)

gold
(jewellery)

copper
(wire)

steel
(tools)

see also alloy, electricity, gold, iron, lead, steel

metamorphic rock see rock

metamorphosis

Metamorphosis is a major change from one form to another, such as when a tadpole changes into a frog.

see also amphibian, caterpillar

meteor

A meteor is a piece of rock entering the Earth's atmosphere at great speed and burning up. We see it as a streak of light across the night sky.

• **Meteors** often come in showers when the Earth passes through dust in space.

see also atmosphere, space

meteorite

A meteorite is a piece of rock which has fallen to Earth from outer space. As it comes through the Earth's atmosphere it is seen as a streak of light we call a meteor.

meteorologist

A meteorologist is a person who studies the weather. Meteorologists can sometimes tell us what the weather will be like in the future.

• Another name for a **meteorologist** is a weather forecaster.

methane

Methane is a gas produced from decaying waste. It is the main part of natural gas.

• *Methane has no colour but it does smell.*

method

Method means the way something is done. There are special methods for investigations and tests to make sure they are done properly.

micro-habitat *see* habitat

micro-organism

A micro-organism is a tiny living creature. Most can only be seen through a microscope. Bacteria, fungi and viruses are all examples of micro-organisms.

• *Yeast is a fungus or a **micro-organism** used in cookery. Yeast makes bread rise.*

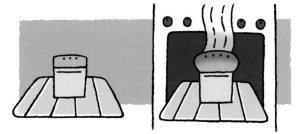

see also bacterium, fungus, germ, mould, virus

microscope

A microscope is a device used to magnify tiny objects.

• *You can see things as small as bacteria through a good **microscope**.*

see also lens, magnify

midnight

Midnight is twelve o'clock at night.

• *Midnight and midday are both twelve o'clock.*

see also day, noon, rotate

midsummer

Midsummer is the time of the year when the Sun is at its highest in the sky, and we have the longest day. Midsummer is another word for summer solstice. The longest day in the northern hemisphere is the 21st of June and in the southern hemisphere is the 21st of December.

see also equinox, midwinter

midwinter

Midwinter is the time of the year when the Sun is at its lowest in the sky, and we have the shortest day. Midwinter is another word for winter solstice. The shortest day in the northern hemisphere is the 21st of December and in the southern hemisphere is the 21st of June.

see also equinox, midsummer

a b c d e f g h i j k l m n o p q r s t u v w x y z

migrate

To migrate is to move from one place to another with the changing of the seasons.

• *Some birds, butterflies, whales and African animals **migrate** to find food every year.*

➤ migration

When a group of animals regularly move of their own will from one place to another it is called migration.

mineral

A mineral is a chemical that occurs naturally. It can be dug out of the ground.

• *Coal, salt and diamonds are all **minerals**.*

see also chemical, natural, rock

minimum

The smallest amount of something is the minimum.

• *The **minimum** temperature ever recorded on our planet was -89°C.*

see also maximum, temperature

mirror

A mirror is a sheet of glass or metal that can reflect an image.

see also concave, convex, image, reflect

mixture

A mixture is a combination of items or substances which can be separated, often by sieving or filtering.

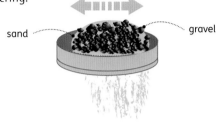

sand .... gravel

see also sieve, filter, change

model

A model is a small-scale representation of an object or a living thing which is much larger.

SKYHAWK

molar *see* tooth

molecule

A molecule is a tiny particle. It is a group of atoms that are strongly attracted to each other.

• *Water molecules are made from two hydrogen atoms and one oxygen atom.*

hydrogen atoms

oxygen atom

see also atom, gas, particle

mollusc

A mollusc is a type of animal with a soft body. A mollusc's body is not divided into segments. It usually has a shell.

• *Molluscs are invertebrates.*

garden snail

blue-ringed octopus

oyster

see also animal, gastropod, invertebrate

momentum

Objects that are moving have momentum. Moving objects need another force to slow or stop them. Heavy objects have more momentum than light objects travelling at the same speed.

• *Fast means lots of momentum: difficult to stop. Slow means little momentum: easy to stop.*

Fast – lots of momentum: difficult to stop.

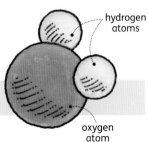

Slow – little momentum: easy to stop.

see also force, friction

Moon (*also* moon)

The Moon is a satellite of the Earth. It orbits the Earth once every 28 days. It is lit by the Sun. Other planets in our solar system have more than one moon.

• *When the Moon is full we see all of one side. At the new moon we cannot see any part of it.*

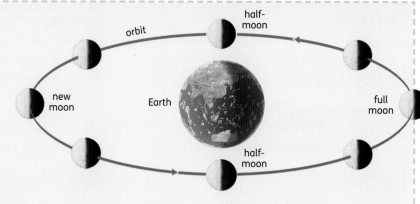

orbit
half-moon
new moon
Earth
full moon
half-moon

the Moon as seen from the Earth

new moon   half-moon   full moon   half-moon

see also lunar, orbit, reflect, satellite

moss

Moss is a small plant that usually grows in wet places. Mosses do not flower. They reproduce using spores.

see also plant, reproduction, spore

motor

A motor is a machine which can make things move.

• *Cars, planes and hairdryers all have a motor.*

mould

A fungus that forms a woolly coating on food, wood or other organic matter is called mould.

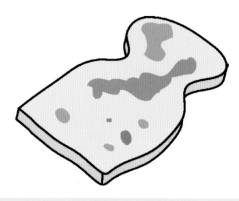

see also fungus, micro-organism

mouth

The mouth is the part of the animal which takes in food.

• *The teeth and tongues of animals are in their mouths.*

see also breathe, food, tooth, tongue

movement

Movement is an act of moving. Animals move from place to place. Plants move their leaves and stems. Machines need a motor or battery to move.

• *The movement of plants involves moving some body parts, such as flowers and leaves, towards the light. Also, their roots move away from light and towards water.*

mucus

Mucus is a sticky slimy substance that protects parts of our body. The insides of our lungs are coated with mucus. Slugs and snails use mucus to help them slide along the ground.

• *When you sneeze, droplets of mucus shoot out of your nose.*

see also lung

mumps *see* childhood illness

muscle

A muscle is a tissue which pulls a part of our skeleton so we can move. The heart is also a muscle.

• *The biceps muscle makes the arm bend. The triceps muscle straightens the arm.*

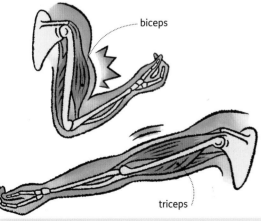

biceps

triceps

see also heart, tissue

mushroom

A mushroom is a type of fungus. Many people eat them.

• *Some mushrooms are good to eat, but many wild mushrooms are poisonous.*

see also fungus

myriapod

Animals with many legs are members of the myriapod group.

• *All myriapods are part of the arthropod group.*

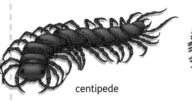

millipede

centipede

see also arthropod, gastropod

a
b
c
d
e
f
g
h
i
j
k
l
m
n
o
p
q
r
s
t
u
v
w
x
y
z

Nn

narcotic

A drug that makes people sleepy is called a narcotic.

SLEEPING PILLS

• *Narcotic medicines can be dangerous. They can only be prescribed by doctors.*

see also drug, heroin, medicine

natural

A natural object or material has not been interfered with in any way by people.

see also manufactured, material

natural gas

Natural gas is produced by the decay of millions of tiny organisms. When the gas is burned it produces not only power for machines, but polluting waste gases as well.

naturalist

A naturalist is a person who studies the natural world and nature.

nature

The term nature covers all living things, landscapes and objects which occur naturally, not those made by people.

➤ nature reserve

In a nature reserve, plants and animals are encouraged to live their lives without interference from people.

• *People may help to protect and manage the numbers and types of plant on a nature reserve.*

nectar

The sweet sticky liquid inside a flower is nectar. It attracts bees, which turn the nectar into honey.

see also flower, honey

negative

Negative means no. The results of a test or experiment are negative if they show that something was not found or that it was not proved.

OPPOSITE The opposite of negative is positive.

see also positive

nerve

A nerve is a long thin tissue that sends messages around our body.

see also brain, tissue

nervous system

The nervous system is all the nerves to and from the senses working with the brain to send messages to the rest of the body. When nerves in the hand touch something hot, a message is sent to the brain about the heat. Another message goes to the hand to move away from the source of the heat.

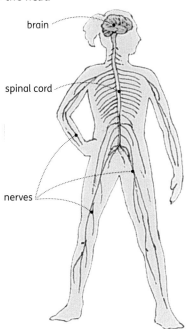

brain

spinal cord

nerves

newton

The unit for measuring force is the newton.

• *The pull of gravity on an average size apple is one **newton**.*

see also force, weight

nicotine

Nicotine is the drug that makes tobacco addictive.

• ***Nicotine** is very addictive. Most smokers want to stop but find it difficult to do so.*

see also addict, drug

night

The time of day when our part of the Earth is facing away from the Sun is night.

• *It is **night** on the unlit side of the Earth.*

see also day, orbit

nitrogen

Nitrogen is the most common gas in the atmosphere.

• *Crisps keep better if there is no oxygen in the bag, so crisp bags are filled with **nitrogen**.*

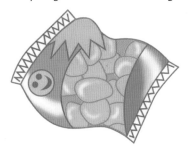

see also air, atmosphere, gas

nocturnal

Animals that are awake during the night are nocturnal. Owls have big eyes to see at night. Many bats use sound echoes to find their way in the dark.

• *Nocturnal animals, like badgers, may have a very good sense of smell.*

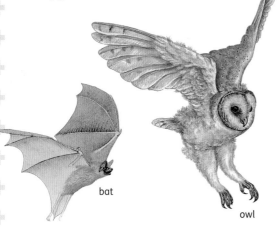

bat

owl

non-flowering plant *see* plant

non-renewable energy
see energy

noon

Noon is at twelve o'clock midday. The Sun is at its highest in the sky at noon.

see also day

north pole *see* pole

nuclear power

In a nuclear power station, heat is produced when an atom's nucleus is broken apart. The heat is used to make steam, which drives the electricity generator.

• *The waste products of **nuclear power** are dangerous for many years.*

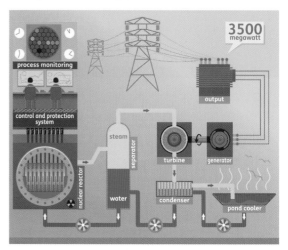

see also atom, nucleus

nucleus (*plural* nuclei)

❶ There is a nucleus at the centre of an atom.

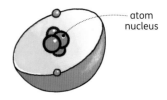

atom nucleus

see also atom

❷ A cell's nucleus controls the way it works.

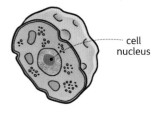

cell nucleus

see also cell

nylon

Nylon is a type of plastic that can be made into strong threads.

• *Nylon threads are used to make clothes and ropes.*

see also inorganic, manufactured

object

An object is a thing which is not alive. It may be a naturally occurring one such as a piece of rock or a manufactured one such as a cup or glass.

see also manufactured

observe

To observe is to watch carefully so as to see something.

➤ **observation**

Observation is watching something carefully so as to see something in greater detail.

ocean

An ocean is a very large area of salt water.

• *The three largest **oceans** on Earth are the Pacific, the Atlantic and the Indian **oceans**.*

oesophagus

The oesophagus is the tube which goes from the throat to the stomach. It is part of the alimentary canal.

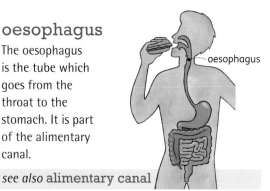

oesophagus

see also **alimentary canal**

oil

Oil is a black sticky liquid that is trapped in rocks underground. It is used to make plastics, petrol, wax and many other chemicals.

• *Refined **oil** is used to reduce friction and make machines run smoothly.*

see also **chemical**

omnivore

An animal that eats both vegetation and other animals is an omnivore.

• *Herring gulls are **omnivores**. They will eat almost anything organic.*

see also **animal, carnivore, herbivore**

opaque

Light cannot pass through objects that are opaque.

• *The glass is transparent, but the boy is **opaque**.*

see also **translucent, transparent**

100

optical fibre

Glass can be made into very thin fibres. These are called optical fibres because light can travel down them. Optical means to do with light or sight.

• *Many telephone calls travel through **optical fibres**.*

see also light

optic nerve *see* eye

orbit

❶ Objects that circle other objects are in orbit around them.

• *Satellites are in **orbit** around the Earth.*

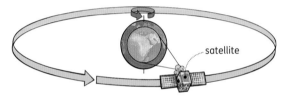

satellite

❷ To orbit an object is to move in an orbit around it.

• *The planets of the solar system **orbit** the Sun.*

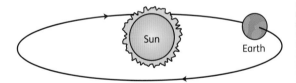

Sun

Earth

ore

Ore is a mixture of rock and metal. It is dug out of the ground.

• *Some rocks contain **ores** which are mined for a mixture of metals. Lead and silver both come from the **ore** called galena.*

see also metal, mineral

organ

An organ is part of the body that does a particular job.

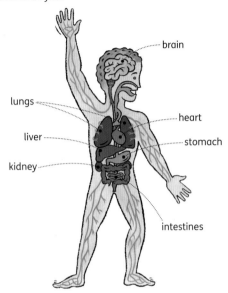

brain

lungs

heart

liver

stomach

kidney

intestines

see also **brain, heart, kidney, liver, lung, stomach**

organic

Anything which is alive or has been alive is organic.

OPPOSITE The opposite of organic is inorganic.

see also inorganic

➤ organic matter

Organic matter comes from plants and animals. All organic matter is alive, or was once alive.

• *Trees and rotten wood are **organic matter**.*

a
b
c
d
e
f
g
h
i
j
k
l
m
n
o
p
q
r
s
t
u
v
w
x
y
z

organism

An organism is a living thing.

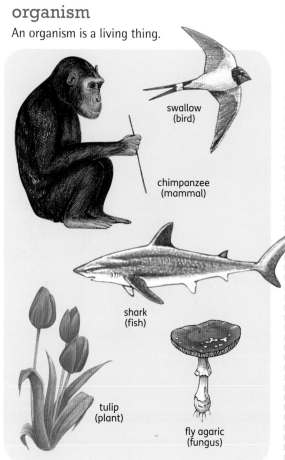

swallow
(bird)

chimpanzee
(mammal)

shark
(fish)

tulip
(plant)

fly agaric
(fungus)

ovary

The ovary is the part of a female animal or flower where eggs are produced.

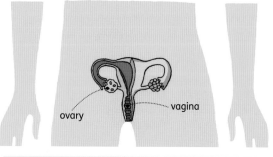

ovary

vagina

see also egg, flower, ovule, womb

ovule

An ovule is an unfertilised seed in a flower. After it has been fertilised it becomes a seed.

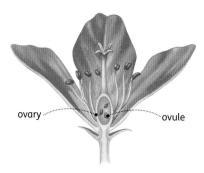

ovary

ovule

see also fertilise, ovary, seed, flower

ovum (*plural* ova)

An ovum is an unfertilised animal egg cell.

• *Ova grow inside the ovary.*

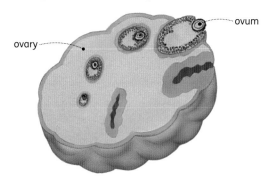

ovum

ovary

see also cell, sperm, uterus, womb, fertilise

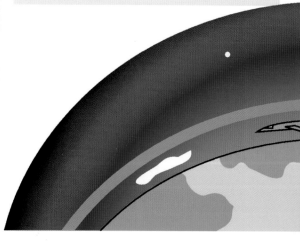

oxide

An oxide is a compound in which oxygen is combined with another chemical.

• *Rusty iron is iron oxide.*

see also compound, iron, oxygen, rust

oxygen

Oxygen is a gas. It makes up about a fifth of the atmosphere. It is vital for living things.

• *Water is a compound of oxygen and hydrogen.*

see also atmosphere, compound, gas, hydrogen

ozone

Ozone is a special type of oxygen. The ozone layer of the atmosphere protects the Earth from dangerous rays from the Sun.

see also atmosphere, greenhouse effect

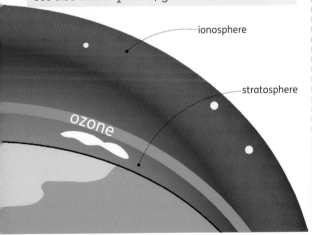

ionosphere

stratosphere

ozone

Pp

palaeontologist

A palaeontologist studies fossils to find out about the past. Mary Anning and Charles Darwin both studied fossils.

• *Some palaeontologists study dinosaur fossils, while others work with the fossils of plants.*

parachute

A parachute is a canopy which can be used to slow something down.

• *Some planes use a parachute to slow them on a runway as they land.*

parallel circuit *see* circuit

parasite

A parasite is a type of plant or animal that gets all its food from another plant or animal.

• *A tick is a parasite that lives by sucking blood from another animal.*

park

A park is a public garden with trees, lawns and plants.

• *In a public **park**, people can play, exercise and enjoy nature.*

see also exercise, garden, nature

part

Part of something is a section of it, not the whole thing.

particle

A particle is a minute piece of what the universe is made from.

see also atom, electron, nucleus

pattern

A pattern is an arrangement of shapes.

• *Bees make cells in a hexagonal **pattern**.*

see also bee

peat

Peat is a crumbly brown material made from partly decayed vegetation. Dried peat can be used as a fuel.

• *Some people grow tomatoes in bags of **peat**.*

see also decay, rot

pendulum

A pendulum is a swinging weight on the end of a piece of string. It is only the length of the string, and not how big the swing is, that affects how fast the pendulum swings.

• *In some old clocks, a* **pendulum** *is used to help keep the clock running on time.*

penicillin

Penicillin is an antibiotic made from a fungus.

• **Penicillin** *kills many of the bacteria that make cuts go septic.*

see also antibiotic, fungus

penis

The penis is the male organ through which urine and sperm are released.

see also genitals, male, organ, sperm, urine

penumbra see shadow

perennial

❶ A perennial is a plant which flowers and lives for many years.

❷ A perennial event happens every year.

period

Women release an egg each month, and if it is not fertilised, they menstruate. The cycle is called a period. Menstruation is called 'having a period'.

see also egg, menstruation, vagina

periscope

A periscope is a device for seeing around corners, or above the water surface from underwater.

• *People in submarines use a* **periscope** *so they can see above the surface of the water.*

see also light, mirror, reflect

permeable

Water can go through permeable materials.

• *A natural sponge is permeable.*

OPPOSITE The opposite of permeable is impermeable.

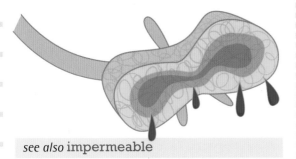

see also impermeable

pesticide

A pesticide is a chemical sprayed onto plants to kill insects and other pests which might damage the plants.

• *When pesticides are overused they damage the environment.*

petal

A petal is the colourful part of a flower which attracts insects to pollinate the flower.

petal

see also flower, pollinate

phenomenon

A phenomenon is a physical event, something which happens.

see also physical

photosynthesis

The way in which plants make food in their leaves is called photosynthesis.

• *The leaf takes in water from the roots and carbon dioxide from the air to make sugar during photosynthesis. It needs energy from light to make this happen.*

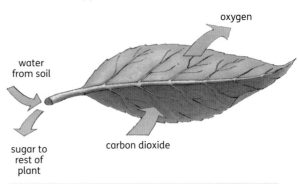

oxygen

water from soil

sugar to rest of plant

carbon dioxide

see also carbon dioxide, plant, sugar, water

physical

Physical events are real ones which can be observed by the senses. Physical objects can be seen, touched, heard, smelled and tasted.

➤ **physical change**

A physical change is one where no new substance is formed. When salt dissolves in water it seems to disappear, but it has not gone from the solution. This is a physical change.

physics

Physics is the study of the non-living world. People who study physics investigate atoms and stars. They look at how things move, and study different kinds of energy, such as light and magnetism.

see also gravity, light

➤ **physicist**

A physicist is a person who studies physics.

• *Physicists ask questions about what causes a rainbow. They want to know why objects fall to the ground.*

pie chart *see* **chart**

pile

❶ A pile is a heap of something.

❷ The pile of a fabric or material is the way the loose fibres lie.

• *The pile on an animal's fur is the way it lies so it can be stroked smooth in one direction but not another.*

pitch

Pitch is a measure of how high or low sound is.

• *High-pitched sounds are screechy. Low-pitched sounds are growly.*

flute

violin

high-pitched

guitar

tuba

low-pitched

see also **sound**

pivot

❶ The place where a lever turns is called the pivot.

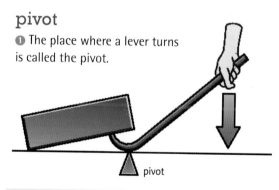

pivot

see also **lever**

❷ To pivot is to turn on a central point, as a lever does.

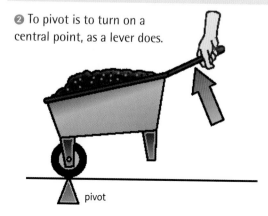

pivot

placenta

The organ that feeds a baby in the womb is the placenta.

• *You were attached to your mother's **placenta** through the umbilical cord. It was attached where your belly button is now.*

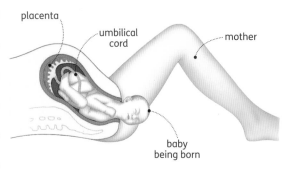

placenta
umbilical cord
mother
baby being born

see also **womb**

planet

A planet is a celestial body which orbits a star. The planets of our solar system are large objects made of rock or gas. They all orbit the Sun.

see also **celestial, orbit, solar**

plankton

Plankton are tiny creatures which live in salt or fresh water. Some are too small to be seen without a microscope.

• *Many creatures that live in the sea eat **plankton**.*

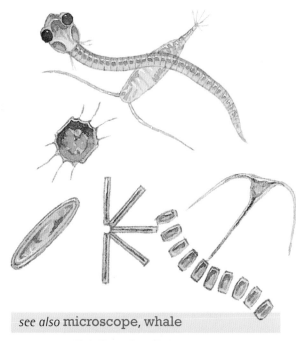

see also **microscope, whale**

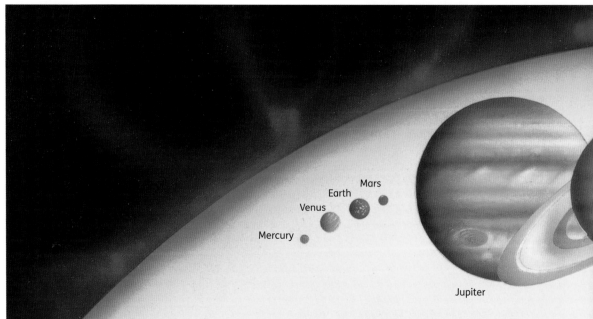

Mercury
Venus
Earth
Mars
Jupiter

plant

A plant is a living thing that uses the Sun's light to make food. Plants grow in the same place all their lives. A plant absorbs water through its roots and uses photosynthesis to create its own food.

• *Trees, ferns, moss, seaweed and flowering **plants** are all types of **plant**.*

see also life, photosynthesis

○ flowering plant

A flowering plant reproduces by making flowers which when fertilised turn into seeds. Roses, potatoes and apples come from flowering plants.

○ non-flowering plant

Non-flowering plants reproduce by using spores. Ferns and mosses are non-flowering plants.

ivy

Sun

Saturn

Uranus

Neptune

plastic

Plastic is a material which is refined from oil and can be moulded when warm. Plastics can be hard or soft.

• ***Plastic** is used to make many things.*

see also manufactured, oil

pneumonia

Pneumonia is an infection of the lungs. It killed many people before antibiotics were invented.

• ***Pneumonia** makes some of the air sacs of the lungs fill with liquid.*

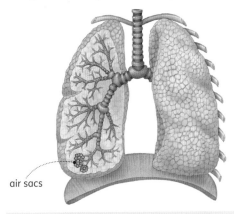

air sacs

see also antibiotic, bacterium, lung

a b c d e f g h i j k l m n o p q r s t u v w x y z

A
B
C
D
E
F
G
H
I
J
K
L
M
N
O
P
Q
R
S
T
U
V
W
X
Y
Z

poison

A poison is a chemical which badly affects or kills a living thing.

• *Snakes inject their poison through hollow teeth.*

see also chemical

pole (*also* Pole)

❶ The end of a magnet is called the pole. It can either be a north or south pole. Unlike poles attract one another. Like poles repel one another.

• *The north pole of a magnet points to the North Pole of the Earth.*

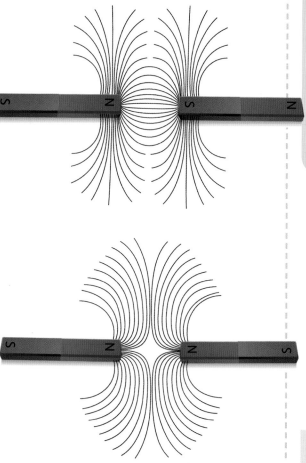

❷ The Earth's poles are the two points on its surface that are at the ends of the Earth's axis.

• *One end of the Earth's axis is the North Pole and the other end is the South Pole.*

see also axis

north pole

The north pole of a magnet attracts the south pole of another magnet. Two north poles repel one another.

south pole

The south pole of a magnet attracts the north pole of another magnet. Two south poles repel one another.

pollen

Pollen is a very fine powder. It is released by the anthers of a flower, which are the male parts. Pollen fertilises the female ovules to make a seed.

pollen

see also allergy, anther, male, ovule, pollinate, fertilise

pollinate

To pollinate is to spread pollen from the male stamens to the female stigma on a flower. This results in fertilisation so the plant can produce seeds.

see also fertilise, flower, pollen

➤ pollination

Pollination may be done by wind or water or by animals, including humans, when they touch both male and female parts of a flower.

➤ pollinator

A pollinator is a bird, animal or insect which pollinates a flowering plant.

• *In the mountains of South America hummingbirds are the main pollinators.*

pollution

Pollution is anything that spoils the environment.

• *Litter causes pollution.*

see also environment, sewage

➤ pollute

To pollute the environment is to spoil it and make it dirty.

• *Untreated sewage pollutes rivers.*

pond

A pond is a small pool of still water which may be natural or made by people.

pool

A pool is an area of still water which is formed naturally.

positive

Positive means yes. The results of a test or experiment are positive if they show that something exists or has happened.

OPPOSITE The opposite of positive is negative.

see also negative

powder

A powder is a mass of dry dust or very small particles.

• *Flour and icing sugar are powders, but granulated sugar is too gritty to be called a powder.*

practical

Something is practical when it can actually be done or made to happen.

precaution

A precaution is something you do to take care.

• *When doing a test you should take precautions to make sure it is done safely.*

precipitation

Precipitation is water that falls to the ground as rain, hail, sleet or snow.

• **Precipitation** *occurs when the droplets in clouds become heavy and fall.*

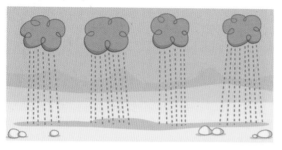

see also **water cycle**

precision

If you do something with precision, you do it very carefully so that it is exactly right.

predator

An animal that catches and eats other animals is a predator.

• *Sharks are ocean* **predators**.

see also **carnivore, prey**

predict

To predict something is to say what you think will happen.

• *It can be interesting to* **predict** *what will happen in a test so that you know how to set it up safely.*

➤ prediction

You make a prediction when you say what you think will happen.

prehistoric

An event is prehistoric if it happened before records began.

premolar *see* **tooth**

present

To present something is to show and explain it.

• **Presenting** *test results should be done in an interesting way. You can use drama and art as well as charts and electronic displays to* **present** *results.*

pressure

Pressure is a force pressing on an area. A force pressing on a small area produces more pressure than the same force spread over a large area.

• *Snowshoes spread your weight over a larger area so that there is less* **pressure** *on the snow.*

prey

An animal which is hunted and eaten by predators is called the prey.

barn owl
(predator)

mouse
(prey)

see also **carnivore, food, predator**

prism

A prism is a shaped piece of glass. It can split white light into the colours of the spectrum.

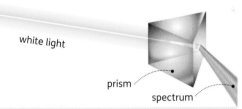

white light

prism

spectrum

see also colour, light, spectrum

process

A process is a series of steps or actions done for a particular purpose.

• *The* **process** *of planning a test includes deciding what you want to find out, how you will do it, as well as how you will measure, record and present your results.*

producer

A producer in the food chain makes its own food. All green plants make food in their leaves from air, water and light.

• *Green plants are the* **producers** *at the start of all food chains.*

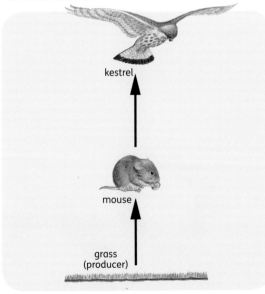

kestrel

mouse

grass (producer)

see also food, photosynthesis, plant

property

A property of something is one of the characteristics it has.

• *Some* **properties** *of wood are that it is hard and strong but flexible and can burn.*

protect

To protect something is to keep it safe from harm.

protein

Protein is essential to build the body's tissues. People need to eat some protein as part of their diet.

• *Meat, fish, eggs, nuts and pulses are good sources of* **protein.**

fish

meat

beans

milk

nuts

eggs

see also diet, food, tissue

puberty

Puberty is the time when children begin to change into adults. Girls begin to menstruate and their genitals get larger. Boys grow face hair, their voices get lower and their genitals get larger. Both boys and girls grow quickly, but boys generally grow bigger than girls.

see also genitals, menstruation

pulley

A pulley is a device for lifting heavy things.

• *Pulleys use a grooved wheel and a rope to raise a heavy load.*

pulse

Each time the heart beats it can be felt as a pulse in the arteries.

• *The resting **pulse** is 75 beats per minute. After running it is 140 beats per minute.*

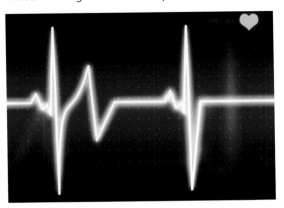

see also artery, blood, heart

pupa (*plural* pupae)

The pupa is the resting stage of an insect between larva and adult.

• *The **pupa** of a butterfly is called a chrysalis.*

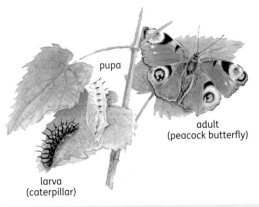

pupa

adult
(peacock butterfly)

larva
(caterpillar)

see also caterpillar, chrysalis, insect, larva

pupil *see* eye

Qq

quartz

Quartz or rock crystal is a very common mineral. A lot of sand is made from quartz grains.

• *Quartz sometimes forms large crystals.*

see also mineral

Rr

radiation

Radiation is energy that can travel through space at the speed of light. Light, heat, X-rays and radio waves are all forms of radiation.

see also cancer, light, heat

radioactive

In some types of atom, the nucleus gives off particles and energy in the form of radioactivity. Materials that give off this kind of energy are called radioactive.

• *Radioactive materials are dangerous. Some of them can cause fatal illness.*

see also nucleus

radius see bone

rainbow

A rainbow is an arch made up of seven colours formed in the sky when sunlight passes through drops of rain. The raindrops act like tiny prisms.

• *Rainbows always appear opposite the Sun.*

see also colour, light, prism

rainforest

A rainforest is a tropical jungle of tall trees and plants which live on them.

• *Rainforests cover only 6% of the world's surface but are home to 50% of the world's plant and animal species.*

see also tree, ecosystem, species

a
b
c
d
e
f
g
h
i
j
k
l
m
n
o
p
q
r
s
t
u
v
w
x
y
z

range

A variety of things of one sort is called a range.

• *A range of people might include those of different heights or nationalities.*

react

When chemicals react they combine together, or split apart, or join up in new ways. This makes new chemicals.

see *also* chemical, change, rust

➤ **reaction**

A reaction is a quick response to a change.

• *If your hand touches a very hot surface, your reaction is to pull it away.*

rear-view mirror

A rear-view mirror allows a person to see what is behind them without turning round.

• *Rear-view mirrors are useful on vehicles.*

see *also* reflect

reason

A reason explains why something has happened.

• *When testing we should look for the best reason for our results.*

see *also* result

record

❶ A record lets people know what happened.

❷ To record information is to keep it so that it can be passed on to others. Recording a result may be done in many ways such as a note, photo or drawing.

• *We record the results of tests so we can see what we have found out.*

recycling

Recycling is the reuse of waste objects and materials.

• *Recycling involves reusing things we no longer need or making them into new objects.*

reflect

To reflect is to show or bounce back an image of something.

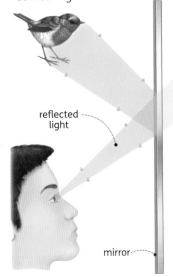

reflected light

image

mirror

➤ **reflection**

A reflection is the image of an object on a shiny surface.

➤ **reflective**

A surface is reflective when it is shiny and reflects an image.

➤ **reflector**

A reflector is a shiny surface which reflects light.

refract

When light is refracted it is bent as it passes from one transparent material to another.

• *Light is **refracted** as it passes from air to glass, and from glass to air.*

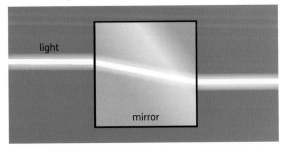

light

mirror

see also light, transparent

renewable

A renewable resource is one which will never run out.

• ***Renewable** resources of energy include solar, water and wind power.*

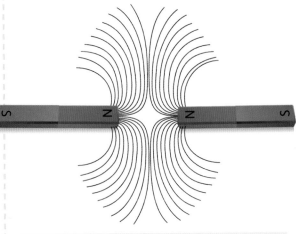

see also solar, energy

renewable energy *see* energy

repel

To repel is to push apart.

• *The like poles of magnets **repel** each other.*

see also magnet

represent

To represent is to let one thing take the place of another.

• *Pictures can **represent** words as headings on a chart.*

a b c d e f g h i j k l m n o p q r s t u v w x y z

A B C D E F G H I J K L M N O P Q R S T U V W X Y Z

reproduction

All types of living things can make copies of themselves. This is called reproduction. There is sexual and asexual reproduction.

○ asexual reproduction

Asexual reproduction does not involve male and female cells. Only one parent is needed. Asexual reproduction occurs mostly in plants and bacteria. It is rare in animals except in a few simple kinds like the worm.

○ sexual reproduction

When animals reproduce sexually, a sperm cell from a male animal combines with an egg from a female to produce a baby. When plants reproduce sexually, the male and female parts of the plant are involved.

asexual reproduction

worm

sexual reproduction

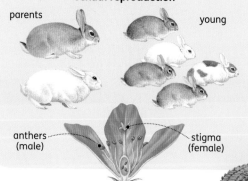
parents
young
anthers (male)
stigma (female)

reptile

Reptiles are cold-blooded animals with dry scaly skin. They lay leathery eggs.
• *Snakes, frogs, crocodiles and turtles are all reptiles.*

see *also* beak, cold-blooded, dinosaur, egg

research

❶ To research is to investigate carefully.
❷ Research is careful investigation of a subject.
• *Research can be done through observation, testing, measuring and recording results.*

see *also* observe, record, test, measure, result

resistance

Resistance is when something opposes another thing.
• *Strands of cotton can be tested to find their resistance to breaking.*

○ air resistance

Air resistance is the force that slows down objects that move through the air.
• *A skydiver falls fast until he opens his parachute. Then air resistance on the parachute slows him down.*

see *also* aerodynamic, parachute

○ electrical resistance

Electrical resistance occurs when an electrical current cannot easily pass through a material. An electrical resistor reduces the flow of electricity in a circuit.

see *also* conduct, current, electricity

○ water resistance

Water resistance is the force which slows the movement of an object through water. Propellers push a boat through water against the water resistance.

crocodile

chameleon

python

respiration

Respiration is the process in which sugar is broken down in the body to give energy. In animals, oxygen is needed to do this and carbon dioxide is excreted.

see also carbon dioxide, cell, energy, excrete, oxygen

➤ respire

To respire is to carry out the process of respiration. Both animals and plants respire.

result

The result of a test is what happens.

retina *see* eye

reversible change *see* change

ribs *see* bone

rock

Rock is a hard natural substance made of mineral which forms the Earth's crust. There are three main categories of rock and many types of rock.

⚙ igneous rock

Igneous rock forms when hot liquid rock from deep in the Earth cools and becomes solid.

• *When lava from a volcano cools, it forms* **igneous rock**.

see also lava, volcano

⚙ metamorphic rock

A metamorphic rock is igneous or sedimentary rock that has been changed by heat or pressure.

⚙ sedimentary rock

Sedimentary rock is formed when sediment collects at the bottom of a lake or sea.

• *The walls of the Grand Canyon are made of layers of* **sedimentary rocks**.

igneous rock

metamorphic rock

sedimentary rock

WORD BUILD

➤ chalk

Chalk is a sedimentary white rock made from very small sea creatures that lived millions of years ago.

➤ clay

Clay is a soft sedimentary rock which can be squashed and moulded into different shapes. It is brittle when dry.

see also ceramic

➤ granite

Granite is an igneous rock which has solidified. The minerals in it are easily seen.

➤ limestone

Limestone is a sedimentary rock made from the bodies of dead sea animals that lived millions of years ago.

➤ sandstone

Sandstone is a sedimentary rock made from compressed sand.

a b c d e f g h i j k l m n o p q r s t u v w x y z

rocket

A rocket is a device that shoots gases out behind it to thrust the machine forward.

root

The part of a plant that anchors it in the soil is called the root. Roots take in water for the plant. Some store water as well.

• *We eat many types of root, such as carrots and turnips.*

see also plant, soil

rot

When a plant or an animal dies, its body begins to fall apart. This process is known as rotting.

• *When materials start to rot, living things such as fungi depend upon them for food.*

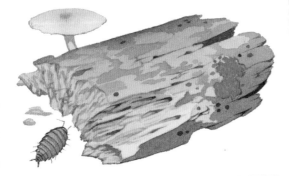

see also decay, fungus

rotate

When an object rotates, it turns on its axis. The Earth turns on its axis once each day.

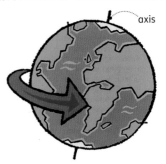

axis

see also axis, day, Earth

➤ rotation

Rotation is turning. Day and night are caused by the rotation of the Earth on its axis.

rust

Rust is iron oxide. It forms when iron reacts with water and oxygen from the air.

• *Iron tools left out in the rain will form rust.*

see also iron, oxide, react

safety

Safety is about protection and preventing accidents.

• *Safety planning is an important part of experiments in the lab.*

salmon

A salmon is a fish which starts life in fresh water but migrates to salt water to breed.

see also **fish, migrate, vertebrate**

salt

The salt we put on our food is a chemical made from sodium and chlorine. It is called sodium chloride.

• *Salt is mined from rocks or extracted from seawater. It forms cube-shaped crystals.*

see also **chemical, crystal, distil**

sand

Sand is tiny pieces of rock which have been worn away by erosion. They are mainly quartz, and may include shells.

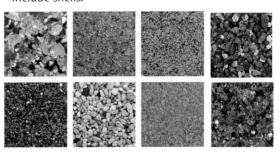

see also **erosion**

sandstone *see* rock

satellite

An object that orbits a planet is called a satellite. Moons are natural satellites. People have made artificial satellites to help with communications on Earth.

• *Hundreds of artificial satellites orbit the Earth.*

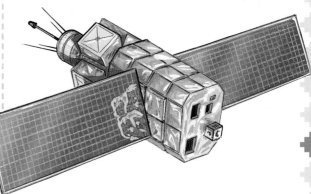

see also **Moon, orbit, planet**

saturated

A solution is saturated when no more solid can be dissolved in it.

see also **dissolve, solute, solution, solvent**

scale

Scales are overlapping plates that cover an animal's body. On fish they are tough, but on butterfly's wings they are very delicate.

• *Fish* **scales** *are made of keratin. Our fingernails are made of the same material.*

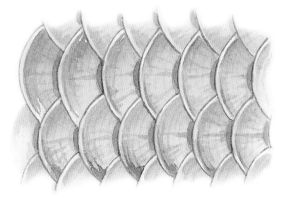

see also fish, reptile

scan

To scan is to look at something carefully.

➤ **scanner**

A scanner is a machine, often used in hospitals, to see inside the body to check for problems.

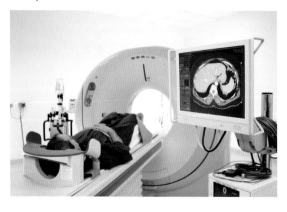

scattergram chart *see* chart

scavenger

A scavenger is an animal which eats dead animals it has not killed itself.

• *Vultures and rats are* **scavengers.**

vulture

science

Science is the study of the natural world.

➤ **scientific**

Studying something in an organised way, making careful observations and measurements, is scientific.

➤ **scientifically**

To work scientifically is to work in a careful and organised way that involves testing ideas, measuring and analysing results.

➤ **scientist**

A scientist is a person who studies science. For example, Rosalind Franklin and Charles Darwin were scientists.

seashore

The seashore is the land beside the sea. It may be covered by the sea at high tide. Living things in a seashore habitat are adapted for life there.

see also adapt, habitat

season

Seasons are periods of similar weather. In places like Europe there are four seasons (spring, summer, autumn and winter), but many tropical areas have two, the wet and the dry season.

• *When the **season** is summer in the northern hemisphere it is winter in the south.*

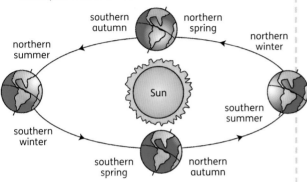

sediment

Sediment is a solid that settles at the bottom of a liquid.

• *After the storm the **sediment** in the river was stirred up, and the river became cloudy and muddy.*

sedimentary rock *see* rock

seed

A seed is the part of a plant which it makes to ensure its reproduction. Seeds develop in the ovary of a flower after it has been fertilised. Seeds germinate to form new plants.

see also reproduction, germinate, ovary, fertilise

seed dispersal *see* dispersal

seedling

A young plant is called a seedling.

segment

A segment is a part or section of something. Arthropods have bodies which are made up of segments.

see also arthropod, mollusc

a
b
c
d
e
f
g
h
i
j
k
l
m
n
o
p
q
r
s
t
u
v
w
x
y
z

semen

The fluid that contains the male sperm is called semen. It is passed to the female during sexual intercourse.

• *Each teaspoon of **semen** contains millions of sperms.*

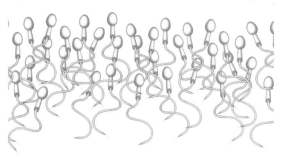

see also **sexual intercourse, sperm**

senses

Humans have five senses: sight, smell, touch, taste and hearing.

• *Animals and people use their **senses** to detect what is happening around them.*

eyes
(sight)

ears
(hearing)

nose
(smell)

tongue
(taste)

fingers
(touch)

sepal

Sepals are the parts of a plant that protect a flower before it opens.

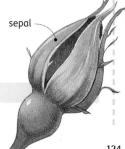

sepal

see also **calyx, flower**

separate

To separate something, parts of it must be placed in different groups.

➤ **separation**

Separation is the act of placing items in different groups.

septic

Something which is septic is infected with harmful bacteria.

see also **infect, bacterium, antiseptic**

series circuit *see* circuit

sewage

Waste water from lavatories and drains is called sewage. It is treated with useful bacteria to break it down and make it harmless.

• *Waste water is treated at a **sewage** works.*

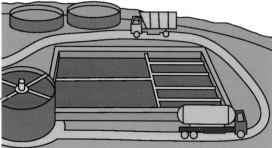

see also **bacterium**

sexual intercourse

In sexual intercourse, the male inserts his penis into the female's vagina. His sperm can fertilise the female's egg to make a baby.

see also fertilise, genitals, penis, reproduction, sperm, vagina

sexual reproduction
see reproduction

shadow

When a light source is blocked by an object, the dark shape behind the object is its shadow.

WORD BUILD

➤ **penumbra**

The penumbra of an object is the outer part of its shadow.

➤ **umbra**

An umbra is a deep shadow.

shape

The term shape refers to the outline or form of something.

• *Looking at the **shapes** of leaves or flowers helps to identify the plant they are from.*

see also identify

sieve

A sieve is a device with a mesh of holes to let small particles through while holding back larger pieces.

➤ **sieving**

The process of separating large particles from smaller ones is called sieving. Sometimes several sieves with different sized holes may be used to sort complicated mixtures.

gravel and sand mixture

sieve

sand

silicon

Silicon is an element. It is used to make silicon chips.

• *Silicon chips are used in things like computers, calculators and smartphones.*

see also element

similar

If two objects are similar they have something in common or are alike in some ways.

• *Two animals may have **similar** markings.*

zebra

zebra fish

➤ similarity

A similarity is what two objects have in common.

• *The **similarity** between two rocks might be their colour or types of crystals.*

simple circuit *see* circuit

skeleton

An animal's skeleton is the framework that supports or covers its body. Vertebrates have an internal skeleton or endoskeleton made of bone. Insects and many other invertebrates have an external skeleton or exoskeleton.

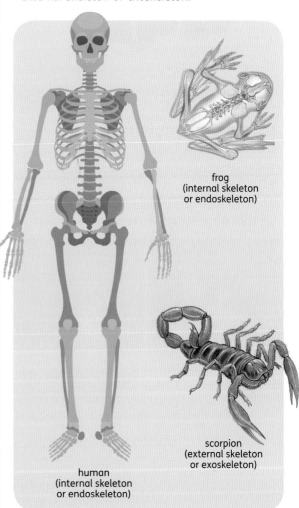

frog
(internal skeleton
or endoskeleton)

scorpion
(external skeleton
or exoskeleton)

human
(internal skeleton
or endoskeleton)

see also bone, invertebrate, vertebrate

skin

The covering of animals is called skin. Mammals have hairy skin. Reptiles and fish have scaly skin. Birds' skin is covered in feathers. The skin of amphibians is smooth and damp.

• *A polar bear has black **skin**! You can see this around its nose.*

see also amphibian, bird, cell, fish, mammal, reptile

skull *see* bone

slug

A slug is an invertebrate which moves on one fleshy foot spreading mucus as it goes.

see also invertebrate, mucus

snail

A snail is an invertebrate which has a shell on its back. The snail can withdraw into the shell in times of danger.

see also invertebrate

snake

A snake is a vertebrate with no limbs. It moves by wriggling.

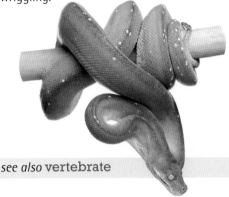

see also vertebrate

snow

Snow is water frozen into single ice crystals. These crystals clump together to form snowflakes.

• ***Snow** falls in the form of snowflakes. Each snowflake has six arms.*

see also crystal, freeze, state of matter

soil

Soil is ground-up rock mixed with plant and animal remains.

topsoil rich in humus

subsoil with little humus

bedrock

see also humus, rock

solar

Solar means to do with the Sun.

see also Sun

➤ solar energy (*also* solar power)

Solar energy is the heat and light which comes from the Sun. It is a form of renewable energy.

see also energy

➤ solar system

The solar system is the Sun and its orbiting planets.

• *We are now discovering that there are many* **solar systems** *in the universe.*

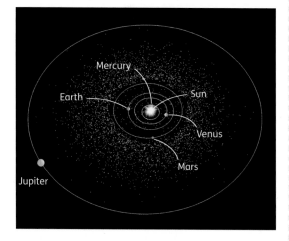

solid

A solid is a substance that holds its shape and is not a liquid or gas.

• *Rocks are* **solids**. *They can be cut or broken.*

see also gas, liquid

solidify

To solidify means to change from a liquid to a solid.

• *Chocolate* **solidifies** *at room temperature, while water* **solidifies** *into ice at 0°C.*

see also freeze, ice

solstice *see* midsummer, midwinter

soluble

Solids and gases that dissolve in a liquid are soluble.

• *Sugar is* **soluble** *in water.*

see also insoluble, solution

➤ solubility

Solubility means whether a substance will dissolve easily in water.

solute

A solute is a solid or gas that will dissolve in a liquid.

• In this solution carbon dioxide is the **solute**.

FIZZY ORANGE

see also solution

solution

A solution is a mixture of a liquid with a dissolved solid or gas.

• Coffee is a **solution**.

see also dissolve

solvent

A solvent is a liquid that will dissolve a solid or a gas.

• Water is not used in dry cleaning. Other **solvents** are used to dissolve grease and dirt.

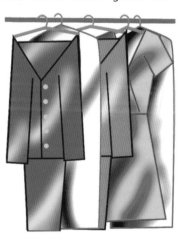

see also dissolve, solution

sort

To sort is to put items into different groups.

sound

Vibrations cause sound. We hear sound with our ears.

• When you hit a drum, the drumskin vibrates and makes a **sound**.

see also vibrate

source

The source of something is where it comes from.

• The **source** of a river may be a spring in the hills.

south pole *see* pole

space

Space is everything outside the Earth's atmosphere. Most of space is a vacuum.

• **Space** probes have left our solar system and are exploring **space** between the stars.

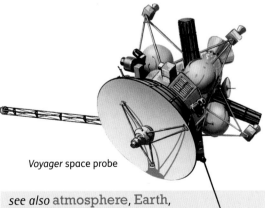

Voyager space probe

see also atmosphere, Earth, solar, star, universe, vacuum

spacecraft

A spacecraft is a vehicle for travelling in outer space.

species

Types of living things are called species. We are the human species. Scientists call our species Homo sapiens.

• *Tigers and cheetahs are two different **species** from the cat family.*

cheetah

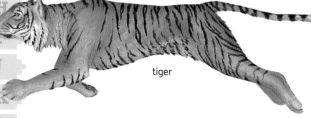

tiger

spectrum (*plural* spectra)

The spectrum is all the colours of the rainbow.

see *also* colour, light, prism, rainbow

speed

Speed refers to how fast something can move.

sperm

Sperm are single cells produced by male animals. Sperm fertilise the female's eggs.

• *A **sperm** cell swims using its tail. **Sperm** cells are tiny compared with the female egg.*

head

collar

tail

see *also* fertilise, male, pollen, semen

spider

A spider is an arachnid, an eight-limbed invertebrate with two parts to its body. Unlike scorpions they have no sting or pincers. They have poisonous fangs instead.

see *also* arachnid, invertebrate

spine

The backbone of vertebrate animals is also called the spine.

• *The nerves of the spinal cord run in a tube up the **spine**.*

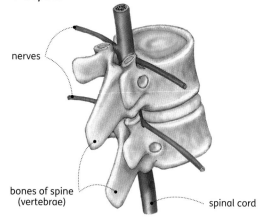

nerves

bones of spine (vertebrae)

spinal cord

see *also* invertebrate, nerve, vertebrate

spore

Spores are like seeds but they are much smaller. Spores are used for reproduction by fungi, bacteria, ferns and mosses.

• *The **spores** produced by fungi make lovely patterns on paper.*

see *also* bacterium, fungus, seed

A B C D E F G H I J K L M N O P Q R S T U V W X Y Z

spring

A spring is a strip of metal which when coiled stores the energy from its twisting. A spring can be stretched but will return to its coiled shape when released.

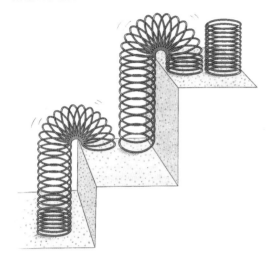

stage

A stage is a part of the life of a living thing.

• *Some plants have a dormant stage when they are not growing. An insect such as a fly has a larval stage when it is a maggot.*

see also maggot, larva, dormant

stamen

The male parts of a flower are called the stamen.

• *The anther and filament together make up the stamen.*

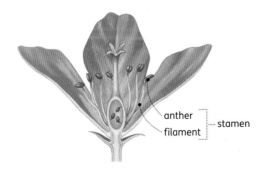

see also anther, flower, male, pollen

star

A star is a huge ball of glowing hydrogen gas. The Sun is our closest star.

• *The stars in the night sky are so far away that they look like points of light.*

see also hydrogen, space

starch

Starch is food that gives us energy. Bread, pasta, maize, cereals and potatoes contain starch.

see also carbohydrate

starfish

A starfish is not a fish. It is a star-shaped invertebrate which lives in the sea and has between 5 and 50 limbs.

state of matter

The state of matter an object is in may be a gas, a liquid or a solid.

steel

Steel is made from iron. Small amounts of other metals or carbon are added to the iron.

• *Many tools are made from hardened steel.*

see also **carbon, iron, rust**

stem

The stem of a plant supports the leaves and flowers.

• *The **stem** of a tree seedling develops into its trunk.*

stem

sterile

Anything that is free from living micro-organisms is sterile.

• *This blade must be **sterile** to avoid infection during an operation.*

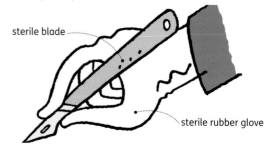

sterile blade

sterile rubber glove

see also **infect, micro-organism**

stethoscope

A stethoscope is an instrument used to hear sounds inside the bodies of people and animals. Sound travels up two hollow tubes to the ears.

• *A doctor uses a **stethoscope** to hear sound inside the lungs and heart. This tells the doctor if the body is working well.*

stigma

The stigma is the top of the female part of the flower. It is sticky so pollen grains get caught on its surface.

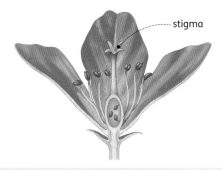

stigma

see also flower, pollen, stamen

stomach

The stomach is a bag in the body in which the digestion of food begins.

• *There is very strong acid in the **stomach**.*

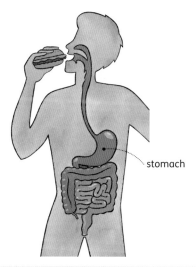

stomach

see also acid, alimentary canal, digest, food

strength

The strength of something is shown by how well it can withstand a force or pressure.

structure

The structure of an object is how it is formed.

subdivide

To subdivide something is to divide it more than once.

submarine

Submarines are ships that can float below the surface of the water.

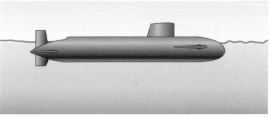

floating

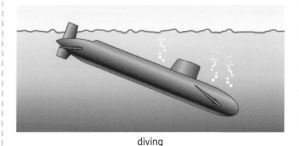

diving

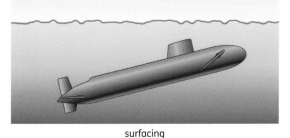

surfacing

see also periscope, upthrust

a b c d e f g h i j k l m n o p q r s t u v w x y z

substance

A substance is a material made of only one type of stuff.

- *Water and salt are both pure **substances**.*

see also material

sugar

Sugar is a sweet food that gives energy. There are several types of sugar.

- ***Sugar** is the main ingredient in sweets.*

see also carbohydrate

Sun

The Sun is the star at the centre of our solar system.

- *The temperature at the **Sun's** surface is 6,000°C but at the core it is 15 million °C.*

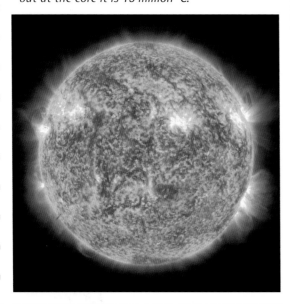

see also solar, star

sundial

A sundial uses the position of a shadow to tell the time. The shadow's position changes as the Sun moves across the sky.

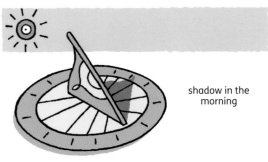

shadow in the morning

shadow in the evening

see also Sun

surface

The surface of an object is its outer part or top layer.

- *When a plane takes off, it rises above the **surface** of the Earth.*

survival

Survival means the way an organism manages to exist despite life-threatening events.

suspension

A suspension occurs when a solid is mixed with a liquid and the particles are dispersed throughout the liquid. The mixture can be separated in a reversible change.

see also change

sustainable

Sustainable describes something that can be kept the same.

• *Sustainable* farming does not wear out the land.

sweat

Sweat is salty water which oozes out of our skin. As it evaporates, it cools our body.

see also evaporate

switch

A switch is part of an electrical circuit that can stop or allow electricity to flow.

• *If you press on this switch it will complete a circuit and turn the light on.*

see also electric symbols

symbol

A symbol is a mark which stands for something else. A number, a letter or an icon can be used as a symbol.

radiation   acid burns   fire

synthetic

Materials that are synthetic have been manufactured. Nylon and glass are both synthetic materials.

see also manufactured, natural

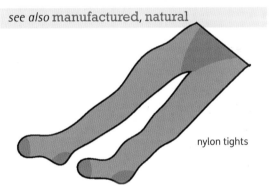

nylon tights

system

A system is a group of items working together.

• *In our digestive system the stomach and intestines work to digest food.*

see also circulatory system, ecosystem, immune system, nervous system

systematic

To be systematic, a task is done in an organised way.

➤ systematically

Systematically means in an organised way.

• *Tests need to be carried out systematically.*

table

A table is a grid of cells in which data can be stored in rows and columns.

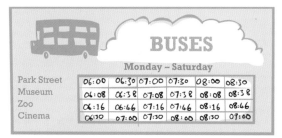

BUSES

Monday – Saturday

Park Street	06:00	06:30	07:00	07:30	08:00	08:30
Museum	06:08	06:38	07:08	07:38	08:08	08:38
Zoo	06:16	06:46	07:16	07:46	08:16	08:46
Cinema	06:30	07:00	07:30	08:00	08:30	09:00

telescope

A telescope is a tube with lenses or mirrors which magnify a distant object.

see also lens, magnify

temperature

An object's temperature is a measure of how hot it is. Temperature is measured in degrees Celsius (°C).

• *Iron melts at a **temperature** of over 1,500°C.*

see also thermometer, Celsius

tendril

A tendril is a thread-like part of a plant which stretches and spirals around supports.

• *Pea plants have **tendrils** which help the plant to climb over other plants and supports.*

test

A test is an experiment to see if an idea is true or not. Factors which affect a test, such as size, time or distance, are called variables.

• *It is important to change only one variable at a time in a **test**.*

see also variable

⚬ **fair test**

A fair test is one where only one variable is changed each time measurements are made.

testicle

Sperm are produced in the testicles.

• *Testicles are held away from the rest of the body to keep them cool.*

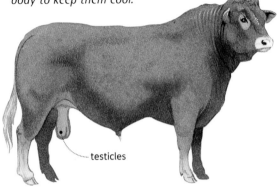

testicles

see also sperm

texture

The texture of an object or material is the way it feels to the touch.

• *It can be important to note whether a leaf has a rough or smooth or sticky or shiny surface texture in order to identify it.*

thermal

Thermal means to do with heat and temperature.

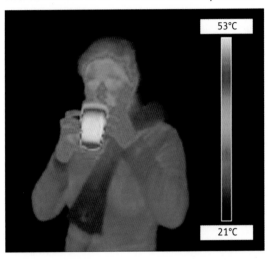

53°C

21°C

thermometer

A thermometer is a device for measuring temperature.

• *Clinical thermometers are used to take people's temperature.*

see also mercury, temperature

thorax

The thorax is another word for the chest.

• *An insect's thorax is the middle part of its body. Its legs and wings are attached to the thorax.*

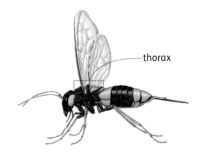

thorax

see also insect

a b c d e f g h i j k l m n o p q r s t u v w x y z

thunder

Thunder is the noise made when lightning flashes from clouds. We hear the sound after we see the light because sound travels much more slowly than light.

see also lightning, sound

tibia see bone

tidal power

Tidal power is the force generated by the rise and fall of the sea tides. This power can be used to generate electricity.

see also energy

tide

The tide is the daily rise and fall of the level of the sea. In many places there are two high tides and two low tides each day. Tides are caused by the gravity of the Moon pulling on the oceans.

• In some places the **tide** only rises and falls once a day.

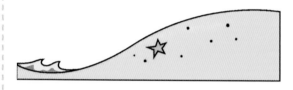

see also gravity, Moon

time

Time tells you how long something takes to happen.

> **WORD BUILD**
>
> ➤ timeline
>
> A timeline is a graphical representation of events which shows the order in which they occurred.

Timeline for evolution

modern day humans

dinosaurs began
245 million years ago

complex life on earth began
540 million years ago

first living things
3,700 million years ago

formation of the Earth
4,600 million years ago

tissue

The bodies of living things are made from tissue of many different types. Muscle tissue, skin tissue and nerve tissue are examples of tissue types.

• *Muscle **tissue** is made up of bundles of tiny fibres.*

muscle fibre

muscle

see also **cell, muscle, nerve, skin**

tongue

A tongue is a fleshy muscle in the mouth.

• *Many animals have a **tongue** which lets them taste food and move it around their mouth. Some snakes have forked **tongues** to taste the air.*

tornado

A tornado is a spiral of spinning air which travels across some flat parts of the world. Tornadoes can do a lot of damage to trees and buildings.

translucent

Translucent materials let through some light, but they are not completely see-through.

see also **opaque, transparent**

transparent

Transparent materials are completely see-through. Clear glass and clear plastic are both transparent.

see also **opaque, translucent**

tooth (*plural* teeth)

A tooth is a hard growth inside an animal's mouth. Teeth grow in different sizes and shapes so they can cut and chew in different ways.

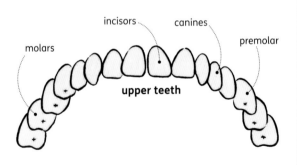

molars

incisors   canines

premolar

upper teeth

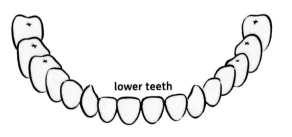

lower teeth

WORD BUILD

➤ canine

Canines are pointed teeth between the incisors and premolars in a mammal. They are used for ripping up food. Carnivores have big canine teeth. Some animals use their canine teeth for fighting.

see also **carnivore**

➤ incisor

An incisor tooth is used to cut food. Rodents like mice and rabbits have prominent incisors to gnaw food.

➤ molar

A molar tooth is used to grind up food in the mouth.

➤ premolar

Premolar teeth grow between the canine and the molar teeth. They chew and grind food. Adult humans usually have eight, two in each jaw on each side.

a b c d e f g h i j k l m n o p q r s t u v w x y z

transpiration

In transpiration, water drawn up by the roots of a plant evaporates off its leaves. As water is lost from the leaves more water is drawn up through the roots.

see also **evaporate**

transport

The term transport refers to any vehicle which carries either passengers or goods.

tree

A tree is a plant which has a single trunk supporting leaves and branches.

• *Trees may be evergreen or deciduous. Some types of tree live for hundreds or even thousands of years.*

see also **deciduous, evergreen**

trunk

The trunk of a tree is its main stem. The trunk is usually covered with a protective bark.

tsunami

A tsunami is a gigantic wave caused by an earthquake under the sea.

• *Tsunami can be very destructive when they reach land.*

typhoon

A typhoon is a large mass of spinning air which brings strong winds and tropical rain to parts of south east Asia.

see also **hurricane, tornado**

Uu

ulna *see* **bone**

ultrasound

Ultrasound is sound that is at a pitch above that which humans can hear.

• *Ultrasound easily passes through skin and muscle. Doctors use it to check on the development of a foetus in the womb.*

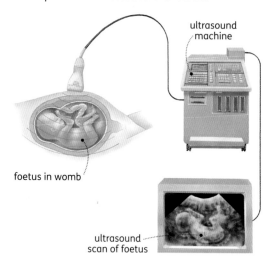

ultrasound machine

foetus in womb

ultrasound scan of foetus

see also **foetus, pitch, sound, womb**

ultraviolet

Ultraviolet is an invisible kind of radiation similar to light. Ultraviolet rays from the Sun turn white people's skin brown.

• *Too much **ultraviolet** can burn the skin.*

see also **ozone**

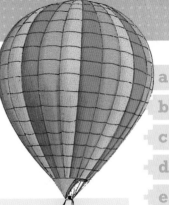

umbilical cord

All the time the foetus is inside its mother she feeds it through the umbilical cord from the placenta. Your belly button is left in the place where the cord entered your body.

• *The **umbilical cord** carries blood containing oxygen and food to the baby.*

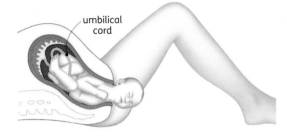

umbilical cord

see also foetus, placenta

umbra *see* shadow

unfamiliar

Unfamiliar means not known well.

universe

There are billions of stars in each galaxy and billions of galaxies in the universe. The universe is everything there is. It is everything we know exists.

upthrust

Upthrust is the force that makes objects float in water or in air.

• ***Upthrust** is greater than the force of gravity on a balloon so it rises.*

see also force

urine

Urine is a mixture of waste chemicals from the body dissolved in water. Urine is excreted by the kidneys and stored in the bladder before it passes out of the body.

see also bladder, chemical, dissolve, excrete

uterus

A baby develops inside its mother's uterus. Another name for the uterus is the womb.

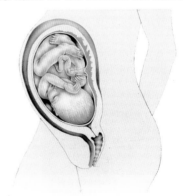

see also vagina, womb

a
b
c
d
e
f
g
h
i
j
k
l
m
n
o
p
q
r
s
t
u
v
w
x
y
z

Vv

vaccinate *see* immunise

vaccine

A vaccine is a substance given to people to give them immunity to an illness.

see also immunise

vacuum

A vacuum is a space that is completely empty. There is no air in a vacuum.

• *Space is a* **vacuum** *so astronauts need to carry air tanks.*

see also space

vagina

The vagina is the female sexual opening. It leads to the womb (uterus).

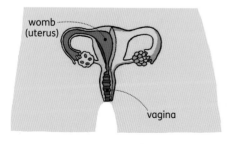

see also genitals, ovary, womb, uterus

vapour

A vapour is a gas. Water vapour is the gas form of water.

• *Water* **vapour** *from the clothes makes the air feel damp.*

see also condense, evaporate, state of matter

variable

A variable is anything you measure in a test.

⚙ dependent variable

The dependent variable in a test is the one which is changed. The scientist measures the results of the change.

⚙ independent variable (*also* controlled variable)

The independent variable is kept the same in each test while you measure the effect of changing other variables. It is also known as the controlled variable.

variation

A variation is a difference.

• *There are* **variations** *between one person's eye colour and another's.*

vary

To vary is to change.

vegan

A vegan is a person who does not eat or use anything from animals.

• *A* **vegan** *diet will not include eggs, cheese, butter or milk.* **Vegans** *do not wear leather, wool or silk.*

vegetarian

A vegetarian is a person who does not eat animals, including fish.

• *A* **vegetarian's** *diet includes milk and egg products and uses nuts, seeds and pulses for protein.*

see also protein, diet

vegetation

The plants that grow in a place are called vegetation.

• *Trees, grass and flowering plants are all types of vegetation.*

see also plant

vein

In many animals, blood is carried back to the heart in thin tubes called veins.

• *You can easily see the veins on the back of an old person's hand.*

see also artery, blood, capillary, heart

verruca

A verruca is a painful wart on the sole of the foot.

vertebra (*plural* vertebrae)

The vertebrae are the bones which make up the backbone in a vertebrate animal.

• *Muscles are attached to the vertebrae.*

see also bone

vertebrate

Vertebrates are animals that have a backbone.

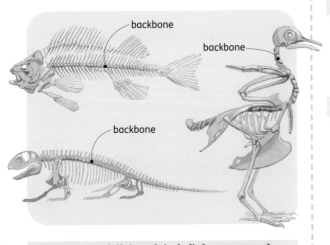

backbone

backbone

backbone

see also amphibian, bird, fish, mammal, reptile, invertebrate

vibrate

An object vibrates when it moves very fast from side to side.

• *Most musical instruments vibrate and the ear hears the vibrations as sound.*

see also sound, ear

➤ vibration

Vibrations are the shaking and tremors from a vibrating object. They may be huge when a volcano erupts or as tiny as the movement of a fly's wing.

virus

Viruses are tiny micro-organisms. They are much smaller than bacteria. They can only live in the cells of other living things.

• *Colds and flu are caused by viruses.*

see also bacterium, influenza, micro-organism

viscous

Viscous means thick and sticky.

• *A viscous substance flows slowly like treacle.*

see also lava, oil

vitamin

A vitamin is a chemical in food which helps the body to stay healthy.

• *Oranges and lemons contain lots of vitamin C.*

see also chemical, food

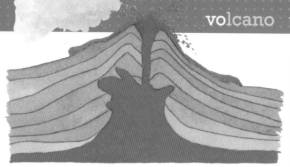

volcano

A volcano is a mountain that has been built up from flows of lava or ash. A volcano that no longer erupts is called extinct.

see also lava, magma, rock

volt

Volts are a measure of the energy of a flow of electricity. Mains electricity carries a voltage of 210–240 volts.

see also electricity, energy

➤ voltage

Voltage is the energy of a flow of electricity measured in volts.

• *Batteries are low* **voltage** *(1.5–12 volts) compared with mains electricity.*

volume

Volume is the space taken up by an object.

• *You can find out what the* **volume** *of a liquid is by using a measuring jug.*

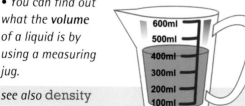

see also density

warm-blooded

Animals that keep their temperature at a constant level are called warm-blooded. Birds and mammals can do this because they have coverings of feathers, fur or fat. This keeps their heat in.

see also bird, cold-blooded, fat, feather, mammal

water

Water is a liquid that is a compound of hydrogen and oxygen. Pure water is transparent, colourless and does not smell. We need about two litres of water a day to keep us healthy.

see also gas, liquid, solid, vapour

➤ water cycle

The water cycle is the never-ending process of water moving from the oceans, up into the atmosphere and back to the Earth and oceans.

see also condense, evaporate

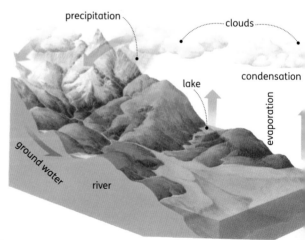

precipitation · clouds · condensation · lake · evaporation · ground water · river

waterproof

A waterproof fabric is one which does not absorb water at all.

• Drops of rain run off a **waterproof** raincoat.

see also absorb

water resistance see resistance

water-resistant

A water-resistant fabric is one which does not easily absorb water.

see also absorb

watt

A watt is a measure of electrical power. A 100 W (watt) light bulb is brighter than a 60 W bulb of the same type. W is the abbreviation of watt.

• A 3,000 **W** kettle boils more quickly than a 2,000 **W** one.

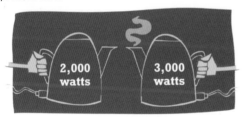

see also current, electricity, volt

weather

Weather is the rain, wind, sunshine, snow or other conditions that you get at a particular time and place.

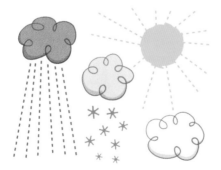

see also climate, precipitation

weight

Weight is the pull of gravity on a mass. In science, weight is measured in newtons.

• The cabbage has a mass of 300 grams. Its **weight** is 3 newtons.

see also density, force, gravity, mass, newton

whale

A whale is a huge mammal which lives in the sea.

• Some large **whales** only eat very small fish and plankton.

see also plankton

wheat

Wheat is a type of grass. People grind wheat seeds to make bread flour.

whooping cough see childhood illness

wind power

Wind power comes from using the movement of the wind to generate power. It is a renewable resource.

see also energy

wire

Wire is a thin thread of metal.

see also metal

a
b
c
d
e
f
g
h
i
j
k
l
m
n
o
p
q
r
s
t
u
v
w
x
y
z

womb

The womb is the organ in females where the baby grows. Another name for womb is the uterus.

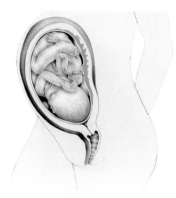

see also female, organ, uterus

wood

Wood is the material which comes from trees.

see also tree

woodland

Woodland is land where trees grow.

see also habitat

work

Work is the ability to make things move or get hot.

• When a crane lifts up a load, it is doing **work**.

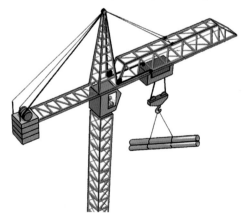

see also energy

X-ray

X-rays are a form of energy that can pass through most materials. They can pass more easily through muscle than through bone.

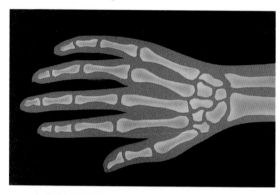

see also bone, skeleton

146

Yy

year

The Earth takes one year to orbit the Sun. A year is $365\frac{1}{4}$ days.

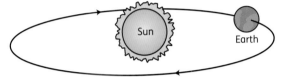

see also Earth, orbit, Sun

yeast

Yeast is a type of fungus. It is a micro-organism that is used in making bread and beer.

• *The carbon dioxide released by* **yeast** *makes bread rise.*

see also ferment, fungus, micro-organism

yolk

The yolk is the yellow part of an egg. It is the food supply for the growing chick.

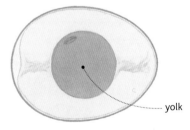

yolk

see also bird, reptile

Zz

zinc

Zinc is a soft silvery-grey metal. It does not rust so it is used to coat steel buckets, lamp posts and crash barriers.

• *When iron is coated in* **zinc** *it is said to be galvanised.*

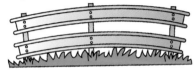

zoology

Zoology is the study of animals.

a
b
c
d
e
f
g
h
i
j
k
l
m
n
o
p
q
r
s
t
u
v
w
x
y
z

Apparatus

Different types of apparatus are used to measure the characteristics of physical objects.

FORCE METER

Spring balances are a type of force meter. We use them to measure the pull of gravity. Force is measured in newtons.

BALANCE

Balances are used to measure the mass of objects. Gram and kilogram masses are put on one side. The object being measured is put on the other side.

TELESCOPE

Telescopes magnify distant objects. The Hubble space telescope gives a view of very distant objects.

THERMOMETER

Temperature is measured using thermometers. Each type of thermometer measures a different range of temperatures. Clinical thermometers only measure temperatures which are close to normal body temperature.

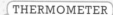

MICROSCOPE

Microscopes show magnified images of tiny objects that are difficult to see with the naked eye.

VOLTMETER AND AMMETER

Voltmeters measure the voltage change between different parts of a circuit. Ammeters measure the flow of electricity around a circuit.

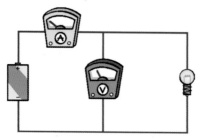

RULERS AND CALIPERS

Length is measured in metres and centimetres. Calipers can measure the diameter of a ball.

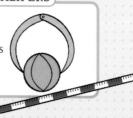

Chemicals

Everything around us is made from chemicals. Chemicals are the building blocks of the universe. The ground beneath our feet, all plants, animals and even people are made from chemicals combined in different ways.

CHEMICALS IN NATURE

Chemicals come in three different forms, solids, liquids and gases.

- Solid chemicals give us iron and gold, while combinations of chemicals give us plants and animals.
- Liquids include mercury and water, which is a combination of chemicals.
- Gases include oxygen, hydrogen and nitrogen.

✳ VOCABULARY BUILDER

substance   waste
material   solid
biodegradable   liquid
combine   pollute
process   gas

CHEMICALS IN THE LABORATORY

People have learned to create different combinations of chemicals, to produce substances they need.

- Medicines such as aspirin come from willow trees.
- Fertilisers and pesticides are made to help us produce more food.
- Fuels are created from oil which is made from naturally occurring chemicals.

CHEMICALS AND THE ENVIRONMENT

Naturally occurring materials such as wool and wood break down easily in the environment. All plastics are made by chemical processes in laboratories and factories. Different forms of plastic are made by using different chemicals. Some plastics are biodegradable but most can take millions of years to break down. Waste materials can pollute and damage the environment.

The History of Life

Planet Earth was formed about 40 billion years ago. At first it was a hot ball of rock and gas on which nothing could live. Life started on Earth more than 3 billion years ago.

The earliest forms of life were probably tiny living things like bacteria. Some scientists say that the earliest life was carried to Earth on a meteorite or comet. Others think that life formed from chemicals on the Earth's surface or deep beneath the ocean.

ONE

Living things have developed into a huge range of types through a process called evolution. Evidence of the way living things have evolved is found in fossils dug out of rocks. Fossils show that there have been changes in living things over millions of years.

TWO

In addition to these gradual changes there have been a few short periods of sudden change. One of these happened 65 million years ago when the dinosaurs and many other types of animals and plants were wiped out in a very short time.

THREE

Humans have made more changes to our planet than any other animal. Some of these changes have altered the habitats of plants and animals. Our buildings take the land on which animals and plants once lived. Some animals have adapted to these changes so that hawks now nest and hunt from skyscrapers while monkeys and foxes have adapted their habits to hunt through city streets.

ferns (*Psaronius*)

winged insects (*dragonfly*)

calamites

LAND

land plants (*Cooksonia*)

harvestman

wingless insects

SEA   trilobites

starfish

sea scorpions

amphibians (*Icthyostega*)

(*Pikaia*)

(*Hallucigenia*)

sea lilies

jawless fish

bryozoans (moss animals)

ammonites

coelacanths

sponges (*Vauxia*)

millions of years ago	500	400

FOUR

There are so many different plants because each has over time adapted to the conditions in which it lives.

Plants called succulents have adapted over thousands of years to changes in climate, by becoming able to store water in their swollen stems.

More recently some plants have been able to thrive near roads where salt has been spread to keep them ice-free.

As we use chemicals to protect our plants, insects needed for pollination are in danger of being destroyed. This could in turn mean fewer plants.

FIVE

Now that global warming, largely due to human pollution, is melting ice sheets and glaciers, plants, animals and people will have to adapt to rising sea levels.

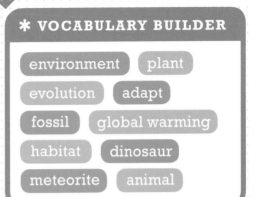

✻ VOCABULARY BUILDER

environment plant
evolution adapt
fossil global warming
habitat dinosaur
meteorite animal

FUN FACT

Before industrial pollution, it was mainly the pale Speckled Moths which survived. When factories left soot on the trees, the darker ones survived. Today, there is less pollution and the pale ones are more common.

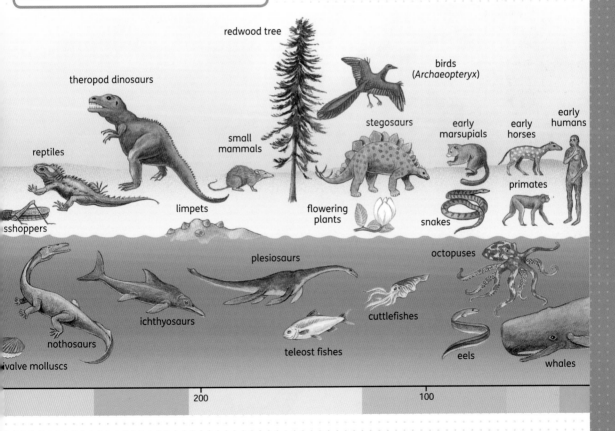

redwood tree

theropod dinosaurs

birds (*Archaeopteryx*)

stegosaurs

early marsupials

early horses

early humans

small mammals

reptiles

primates

limpets

flowering plants

snakes

sshoppers

plesiosaurs

octopuses

ichthyosaurs

cuttlefishes

nothosaurs

teleost fishes

eels

whales

ivalve molluscs

200   100

Classification of Animals

The animal kingdom can be divided into vertebrates and invertebrates. Vertebrates are animals that have backbones, such as fish, reptiles, and mammals. Invertebrates are animals that do not have backbones.

Vertebrates are all more closely related to each other than to other animals, so they are a proper scientific grouping. However, invertebrates are not a proper scientific grouping because the different types of invertebrate are not closely related to each other.

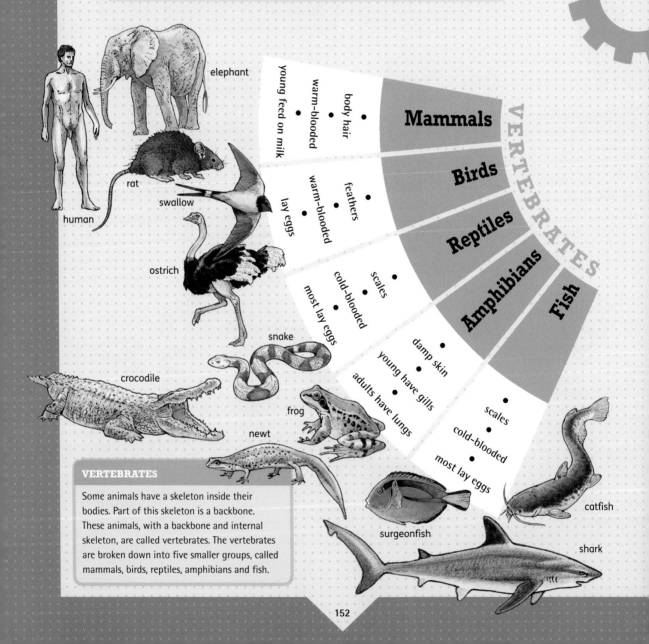

elephant

human

rat

swallow

ostrich

snake

crocodile

frog

newt

surgeonfish

catfish

shark

Mammals
- young feed on milk
- warm-blooded
- body hair

Birds
- lay eggs
- warm-blooded
- feathers

Reptiles
- most lay eggs
- cold-blooded
- scales

Amphibians
- damp skin
- young have gills
- adults have lungs

Fish
- scales
- cold-blooded
- most lay eggs

VERTEBRATES

VERTEBRATES

Some animals have a skeleton inside their bodies. Part of this skeleton is a backbone. These animals, with a backbone and internal skeleton, are called vertebrates. The vertebrates are broken down into five smaller groups, called mammals, birds, reptiles, amphibians and fish.

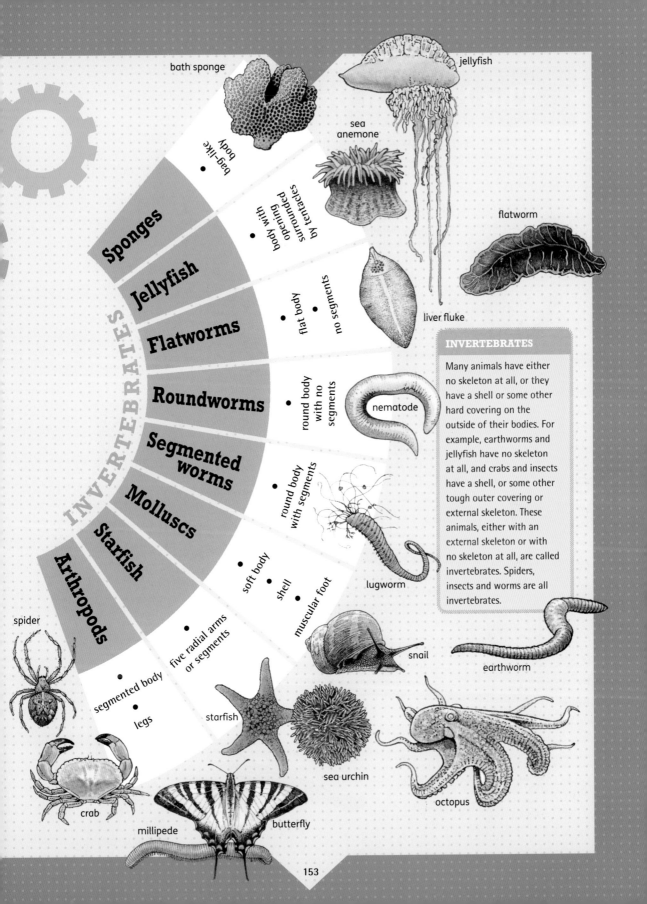

bath sponge

jellyfish

sea anemone

flatworm

Sponges

Jellyfish

Flatworms

Roundworms

Segmented worms

Molluscs

Starfish

Arthropods

INVERTEBRATES

- bag-like body

- body with opening surrounded by tentacles

- flat body
- no segments

liver fluke

- round body with no segments

nematode

- round body with segments

- soft body
- shell
- muscular foot

lugworm

- five radial arms or segments

- segmented body
- legs

snail

earthworm

spider

starfish

sea urchin

octopus

crab

millipede

butterfly

INVERTEBRATES

Many animals have either no skeleton at all, or they have a shell or some other hard covering on the outside of their bodies. For example, earthworms and jellyfish have no skeleton at all, and crabs and insects have a shell, or some other tough outer covering or external skeleton. These animals, either with an external skeleton or with no skeleton at all, are called invertebrates. Spiders, insects and worms are all invertebrates.

The Human Body

The human body is made up of a number of different systems. Each system does a special job.

SKELETAL SYSTEM

The skeleton holds up the rest of the body and protects organs such as the heart and brain.

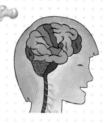

CIRCULATORY SYSTEM

The circulation of blood takes food and oxygen to the body's cells, and takes away waste products.

URINARY SYSTEM

The kidneys clean waste from the blood. The waste passes out of the body in the urine.

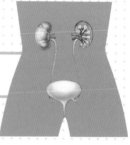

NERVOUS SYSTEM

The nervous system senses the environment and passes messages and commands around the body.

DIGESTIVE SYSTEM

The digestive system takes in food and breaks it down ready for use by the body.

MUSCULAR SYSTEM

Muscles pull on the skeleton enabling us to move.

Parts of the body

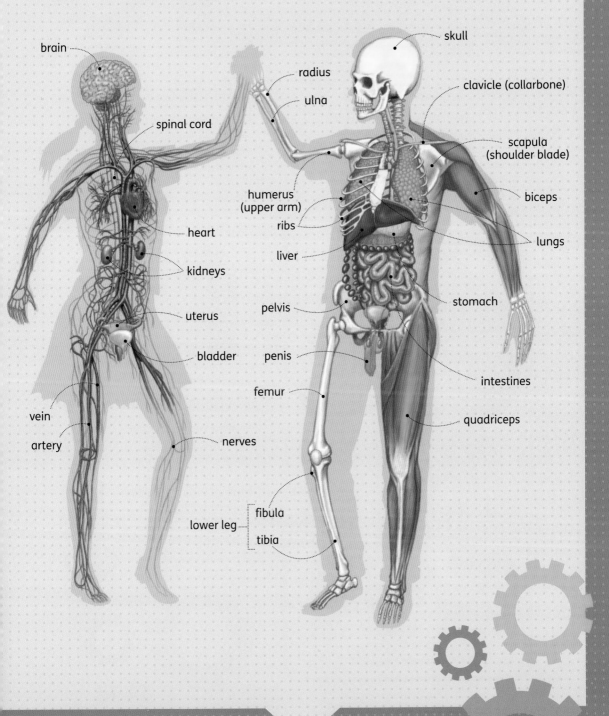

brain

radius

ulna

spinal cord

skull

clavicle (collarbone)

scapula
(shoulder blade)

humerus
(upper arm)

heart

kidneys

uterus

bladder

ribs

liver

pelvis

penis

biceps

lungs

stomach

intestines

femur

quadriceps

vein

artery

nerves

lower leg

fibula

tibia

Energy

There are many forms of energy. Moving things have energy. Energy is what makes everything happen. It cannot be created or destroyed but it can be changed from one form into another. It can be stored in a variety of forms such as a battery or in a fuel. Energy is measured in joules.

KINETIC ENERGY

Kinetic energy is movement energy or the energy produced by movement. An object which is moving vertically or horizontally has kinetic energy. This energy may be supplied by fuel or a push from another object.

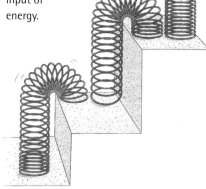

POTENTIAL ENERGY

Potential energy is energy stored in a spring or by raising something up a slope so that it can move down the slope without an extra input of energy.

CHEMICAL ENERGY

Chemical energy is released when there is a chemical reaction. The burning wax of a candle changes the chemical energy in the wax into heat and light.

✳ VOCABULARY BUILDER

natural   atom   joule

radiation   power   fuel

reaction   battery

kinetic   electricity

ELECTRICAL ENERGY

Electrical energy is a form of stored energy which can be changed into heat, light and movement energy.

NUCLEAR ENERGY

Nuclear energy is released when atoms are split or fused together. The heat produced when this happens can be used in a nuclear power plant to make electricity.

LIGHT ENERGY

Light energy enables us to see things. It is the only form of energy we can see directly. Natural light energy comes from the sun through radiation. Light energy may also come from electricity or burning fuel or candles.

HEAT ENERGY

Heat energy is felt as warmth. The Sun supplies energy in the form of heat and light. Geothermal energy is a form of heat energy which comes from the ground.

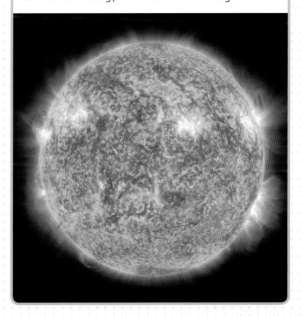

Space and the Solar System

People have long dreamed about exploring space and travelling to other worlds. Space starts 100 kilometres (62 miles) above the surface of the Earth. Earth is one of the planets in our solar system, which is made up of the Sun, the eight planets and their moons. The planets and moons were formed about 4.5 billion years ago at about the same time as when the Sun came into being. The inner planets of Mercury, Venus, Earth and Mars are small and rocky. The outer planets are all much larger and made mostly of gas.

SPACE EXPLORATION

In the last 60 years, unmanned probes have been sent from Earth towards every planet in the solar system, as well to some asteroids and comets. Unmanned rovers have driven over the surface of the Moon and Mars. Telescopes have been launched into space and sent back pictures of distant galaxies. The most famous spacecraft were the five Space Shuttles. Between them they flew 135 missions into space.

INTERNATIONAL SPACE STATION

A spacecraft must travel at 11,000 miles per hour to get into orbit around the Earth. Space stations have been sent into space where astronauts can live and work for several months before retuning safely to Earth. The International Space Station is the biggest of those and can hold a crew of 6 people.

There is no air in space, so astronauts have to take air with them from Earth so that they can breathe. There is so little gravity in the orbit around the Earth that astronauts in the space shuttles or on the International Space Station float in the air. This is called weightlessness. Out of billions of people who live on Earth, only 535 have been into orbit, and only 12 have walked on the Moon.

1957

The Soviet Union sent a satellite called Sputnik into space which was the first to orbit the Earth.

1961

Russian astronaut Yuri Gagarin was the first human being to go into space.

1969

Human beings landed on the Moon for the first time. American astronaut Neil Armstrong was the first person to walk on the surface of the moon.

Uranus

Neptune

Mercury Venus Earth Mars Jupiter Saturn Uranus Neptune

Solar System facts

Planet	Diameter (km)	Number of moons	Average distance from Sun (million km)	Time taken to orbit Sun
Mercury	4,878	0	58	88 days
Venus	12,104	0	108	225 days
Earth	12,756	1	150	365 days
Mars	6,976	2	228	687 days
Jupiter	142,984	16	778	12 years
Saturn	129,660	24	1,427	30 years
Uranus	51,118	21	2,860	84 years
Neptune	49,532	8	4,500	165 years

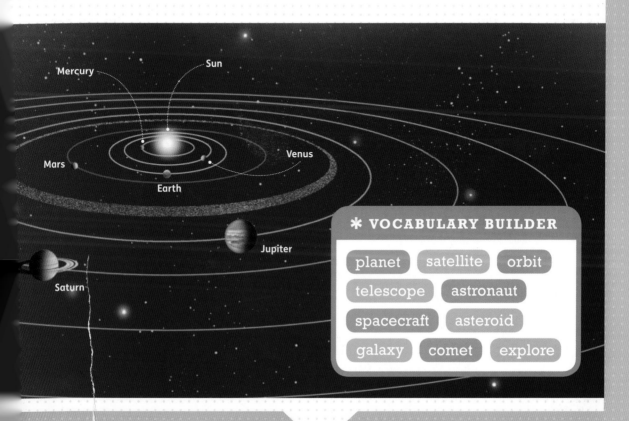

✳ VOCABULARY BUILDER

planet   satellite   orbit

telescope   astronaut

spacecraft   asteroid

galaxy   comet   explore

For more vocabulary and language skills:

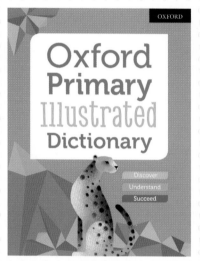

age 8+

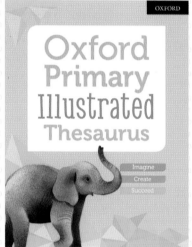

age 8+

age 8+

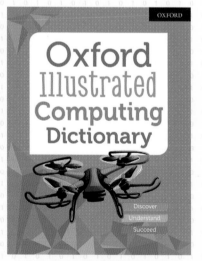

age 8+